Prosper Bender

Literary Sheaves, or, La Littérature au Canada Français

The Drama, History, Romance, Poetry, Lectures, Sketches, etc.

Prosper Bender

Literary Sheaves, or, La Littérature au Canada Français
The Drama, History, Romance, Poetry, Lectures, Sketches, etc.

ISBN/EAN: 9783337008727

Printed in Europe, USA, Canada, Australia, Japan

Cover: Foto ©Thomas Meinert / pixelio.de

More available books at **www.hansebooks.com**

IN PRESS BY THE SAME AUTHOR.

Will shortly appear, "OLD AND NEW CANADA," a work designed to recall the leading incidents of the life of a philanthropist, the late Joseph-François Perrault, and to give some idea of the old French *régime* and life in Canada after the cession, adventures in the Far West and South, social experiences, benevolent enterprises, and educational and other efforts. It will also contain interesting descriptions of Montreal and Quebec and of the favorite scenic localities in the neighborhood of Quebec, etc., etc., etc.

LITERARY SHEAVES,

OR

La Littérature au Canada Français

THE DRAMA, HISTORY, ROMANCE, POETRY, LECTURES, SKETCHES, &C.

BY

P. BENDER, M.D.

> Speak of me as I am, nothing extenuate.
> Nor set down aught in malice.
> *Othello.*

Montreal:
DAWSON BROTHERS, PUBLISHERS.

1881.

Entered according to Act of Parliament of Canada, in the year 1881,
by P. BENDER, M.D.
in the office of the Minister of Agriculture.

Printed by the GAZETTE PRINTING COMPANY, Montreal.

TO THE

HONORABLE WILLIAM WARREN LYNCH,

*Queen's Counsel, Solicitor General of the Province
of Quebec, Member for Brome.*

A TRUE FRIEND OF EDUCATION, AN EARNEST WORKER
IN THE CAUSE AND A MAN OF BROAD VIEWS
AND KINDLY FEELINGS TOWARDS ALL
RACES AND CREEDS, THIS WORK
IS WITH MUCH FRIENDLY
REGARD INSCRIBED.

THE AUTHOR.

LITERARY SHEAVES

OR

LA LITTÉRATURE AU CANADA FRANÇAIS.

"Le style est l'homme même."
—*Buffon.*

THE history of the education of any people perhaps furnishes the best test of its progress and civilization. No wonder, therefore, that the patriotic in all lands display a deep interest in this subject, and cheerfully recommend and make sacrifices for the proper instruction of their fellow-subjects. Our own province supplies a good example of the truth of this remark, with results in every way gratifying. The advance of education in Quebec in the last decade has been remarkable, and the coming census will show very creditable improvement in this respect. Our people have borne, for their circumstances, what may truthfully be described as onerous burdens for the spread of education, and have already enjoyed the satisfaction of reaping substantial fruits from their labors and sacrifices. In this disposition, and with such laudable objects, it is not strange that the subject of compulsory education should have received, especially of late, no little consideration. From a careful survey of the results of this system in other lands, and deep reflection upon the peculiar conditions and needs of their own country, they have largely come to the conclusion that a system of obligatory education is called for at an early day. Nor is there any apparent reasonable obstacle to such an experiment as regards the limited, or defective, character of our present educational system, in all the provinces of the Dominion, particularly in Quebec and Ontario, which have enjoyed an efficient educational machinery for over forty years, annually improving in quality and being administered by agents constantly gaining experience. As to the nature of the means to be employed in the several provinces to accomplish this object, there are perhaps differences of opinion; but there seems, from all that the careful reader of newspaper literature of the day can observe, a general agreement that it is both injudicious and improper to allow any section of the community to grow up in ignorance, a prey to all the vices and evils to which such a condition opens a wide and ready door. In Ontario, for years, the principle of compulsory education has been applied with the very best results. Every important district is familiar with the countenance and labors of the truant officer, whose influence is usefully felt, not only by the wayward pupil, but by his negligent relatives. Nobody now denies either the doctrine of the duty of the State towards all its subjects, or the elevating and steadying character of the instruction of youth. The example of Prussia, in the establishment of such a system, which has been followed by other European countries to a greater or less extent, the latest being England and France, is so far highly satisfactory, as is also their united experience. The same may be said of some of the States in the neighboring Republic, which have acted for years in a similar direction. Any possible doubts on this subject could not last a moment's reflection from the advanced and ever advancing character of the States, which have bent their energies to this great social and moral improvement. It is almost certain that its early adoption by every province of our Dominion will create equal satisfaction, both in a moral and mental point of view.

My object in publishing the following series of reviews is of a twofold character; not only to make the English reading public acquainted with the merits and resources of French-Canadian literature, but also to excite a friendly mutual interest on the part of the different elements of our population, which can be promoted only by a more thorough knowledge of each other. It is very creditable to the national feeling evoked by Confederation that our annals and social circumstances are becoming subjects of absorbing interests to all inquiring minds in the different provinces.

Though my leisure is limited, I have been persuaded to undertake an analysis of French-Canadian literature, as published under the auspices of the Department of Public Instruction, in order to enable the English reader to judge of the spirit and character of a literature, declared by able Frenchmen to be an honor to the intelligence and taste of the nineteenth century. The only regret I feel, in connection with this subject, is the insufficiency of time at my disposal to convey an adequate idea of its high and varied merits, whether grave historical events or dramatic and poetic conceptions be dealt with. French-Canadian literature exhibits a style and animation worthy of the most cultivated writers, and there is the more satisfaction in noticing its development from the fact that, though too little recognized and appreciated by the British element which mingles with our social life, it is generally free from any feeling of prejudice or acerbity, and is evidently inspired by a desire to render justice to every writer, who has contributed to build up the literary honor and interest of the country, as well as to every subject and event deserving of commemoration.

The project of encouraging native literature, inaugurated by the Honorable Gédéon Ouïmet, in 1873, whilst Minister of Public Instruction, and continued by him since his advent to the office of superintendent of that department, deserves more than passing mention. Abandoning the stereotyped method of the importation of foreign books, for bestowal as prizes to the successful pupils of our various schools, that gentleman bethought himself of encouraging native talent by selecting works marked by their originality and ability, and already received with favor by the public, as premiums for the encouragement of the pupils. The object was in every sense patriotic, and the results have justified Mr. Ouïmet's motives and anticipations. Canadian writers, formerly less encouraged than they should have been, were obliged to wait longer for that practical success, to which the great majority of literary men look forward with concern, manifested their appreciation of these opportunities by closer attention to the character of their works by the improvement of previous editions, and greater ambition generally to excel in the domain of letters than had been hitherto evinced. The numerous works of fancy, history and criticism, which have issued from the press within the last few years, attest the value of this patriotic stimulus, no less than the sterling qualities of the authors. This is a new departure, worthy of all praise, and the good fruits of which in great abundance may be hereafter confidently looked for. The change will never cease by an appreciative public to be associated with the name of a gentleman who, from his learning, zeal for public instruction and patriotic ambition, was the worthy source of so excellent an idea. With regard to the practical operation of the new scheme, it may be stated that abbreviated editions of the works of writers of note in the province, of every race, creed and party, have been purchased and distributed as prizes among the scholars; in this way benefiting alike our poorly remunerated authors and our young folk, by placing in the possession of the latter these abridgments, which, in many cases, comprise choice specimens of literature and history. Last year the department distributed, in this way, 14,868 French and 3,790 English works.

It is desirable to afford the public some opportunity of judging of these Canadian works, which have been thought worthy of official selection for the purpose above mentioned, and also on account of their own intrinsic merits. It is but right to admit, at the outset, that an adequate idea of their value cannot always be conveyed through the medium of translation, or by criticism, however carefully and candidly performed. One of the chief objects of the author of these sketches is to furnish the public, unacquainted with the French language, or prevented by the pressure of business, or occupation from a proper study of these works, a fair and sufficient synopsis, to enable it to form a correct opinion with regard to their subjects, merits and style. Another object is the awakening of sufficient interest in those creditable labors to encourage their study by the community generally, French as well as English, and the enlightenment of strangers with respect to the nature and character of our more recent French-Canadian literature.

I propose to notice our different Canadian authors in their order of seniority, without regard to their well earned popularity, both at home and abroad, and before later meritorious works appeared.

HON. PIERRE J. O. CHAUVEAU.

The name of Mr. Chauveau will ever be held in high respect by all acquainted with his character and his services to the cause of public education in the province of Quebec. By his learning and ability he had won a leading position in the political world before particularly identifying himself with that cause ; but his acceptance of the appointment of Superintendent of the Department of Public Instruction, at the time and afterwards, was regarded by those who knew him as a most appropriate course, and fraught with hopes of the best results. Mr. Chauveau, it was felt, had accepted a suitable and congenial mission, in which he could find ample scope for his well-trained intellect and benevolent aspirations. The contest with ignorance, and the extension of the blessings of education form a noble work, in which he who gains even moderate success establishes a title to the gratitude of his countrymen. No man, who compares the state of education in Lower Canada, when Mr. Chauveau first entered upon his duties, with its condition when he resigned, can help acknowledging the great strides it had made in the interval and the improvement in the system of public instruction, in the standard and usefulness of school-books and in the general facilities for the imparting of information. Vigorous efforts had been made to substitute good and productive for old and sterile methods of teaching, and in all essential respects to keep pace with the most progressive countries in the spread of popular enlightenment. It is but candid, however, to admit that greater results might have been achieved, and that education might have been considerably further advanced in this province than it is at this day. Fairness, at the same time, compels the admission that want of means, exceptional social circumstances and physical difficulties connected with our climate, and numerous sparsely settled areas, are largely accountable for the existing deficiencies. Wealthy, thickly settled districts, enjoying easy communication and more moderate winters, and whose people are less isolated from the great centres of modern thought and enterprise, possess advantages in respect to the encouragement of their school systems but slightly experienced in a country like Quebec, many of whose older rural inhabitants, unacquainted themselves with the benefits of education, have not been able to appreciate them in the interest of their children. It is also but right to notice, in this connection, the satisfaction which Mr. Chauveau has generally given the Protestants of Quebec in his administration of that important department. No complaints of prejudice or partiality have been proved against him; on the contrary, he ever seemed to evince as great satisfaction at the progress of the McGill, Lennoxville and other Protestant scholastic institutions, as if a member of the minority himself. His judicious counsel, his presence at examinations, and his desire to encourage their educational efforts have always been available, and with the best moral and material results. The minority had long regarded him as an able, liberal-minded friend, and no section of the community more deeply regretted his retirement from the Education Department. His successor, the Hon. Gédéon Ouîmet, appears desirous of following in his footsteps, and with good results so far, and better yet may be looked for.

L'Instruction publique au Canada, by the above gentleman, was, with the exception of the two last papers, published in Germany some years ago, in the *Encyclopädie des gesammtem Erziehungs und Unterrichtswesens*, edited by Dr. Schmid, of Stuttgart, who had, at the time of a visit paid by Mr. Chauveau to him, extracted a promise that he would write an article on Canada for the second edition of his Encyclopædia, which pledge Mr. Chauveau was called upon to perform in March, 1874 It need hardly be stated that there is no one more capable of doing justice to this subject; it is an elaborate, reliable and complete history of Canadian education. Mr. Chauveau in this performance, brought to his aid vast experience as a director of education, evincing marked grasp of thought and versatility of expression.

The introduction to the volume gives a sketch of the extent of the Dominion, and refers to the clauses of the British North America Act affecting the religious minorities of the two provinces of Ontario and Quebec, rendering them independent of their respective majorities.

Ontario is first treated of by the author, and, in an exhaustive manner, he places before the reader an accurate description of the state of education in that province, beginning with the Department of Education, and continuing with the High, Normal, Model and Primary Schools, including Common and Separate Schools and public libraries; giving the salaries of superintendents, inspectors and teachers of different grades, male and female, the system of internal economy, the *curriculum* followed in each case, and the grants by government, with a comprehensive history of the rise and progress of education. The total sum paid by Ontario for educational purposes in 1874, amounted to $3,587,951.

To the province of Quebec Mr. Chauveau devotes a large part of his work. He begins with the introduction of education by the priests accompanying the first settlers; the foundation by eminent men and women of educational institutions, such as the Jesuits' College in 1637, the Ursuline Convent in 1639, Convent of the Congregation de Notre Dame of Montreal in 1653, the Seminary of St. Sulpice, in 1647, the Grand Séminaire of Quebec in 1663, and the Pétit Séminaire in 1668. At the cession there were few institutions besides the above, and primary instruction for boys was difficult of access, and this state of things continued till 1801, when was created, by Act of Parliament, " The Royal Institution," for the purposes of education, but, according to the evidence of competent people, it was not successful.

The report of the Secretary, the Rev. Mr. Mills, states that in 1834 there were but twenty-two schools, with 398 free and 590 paying pupils, inclusive of 202 pupils of the school superintended by Mr. Marsden, the father of our esteemed fellow-citizen, Dr. Marsden, and 150 of Mr. Holmes' school in Montreal. Fabrique Schools about this time were inaugurated for the Roman Catholics, and in 1836-37 were first instituted the Normal Schools, while extensive private schools were established at Nicolet, St. Hyacinthe, Ste. Thérèse, L'Assomption and Ste. Anne. An excellent school at Quebec, under Dr. Wilkie, was productive of good results at that time, some of our most prominent citizens sending their children to it. " The Society of Education," under the control of Catholic ladies and gentlemen, was founded in 1821, and its first president was Mr. Joseph François Perrault, of whom Mr. Chauveau says : " This distinguished philanthropist operated independently, and founded schools in which he introduced the ' Lancastrian system,' and instruction in arts and trades; he also published, at his own expense, a great number of school-books." In another passage, Mr. Chauveau places this gentleman in the first rank among the pioneers of lay education of this province, and says that " he published, besides the books above mentioned, treatises on jurisprudence, agriculture, history of Canada, &c." And he might have added that Mr. Perrault erected these schools, and paid the teachers thereof, mostly at his own cost ; and that, besides the rudiments of a good education, the boys were instructed in gardening, joinery and the manufacture of agricultural implements ; and the girls in sewing, knitting, carding, spinning and weaving ; and for those purposes he supplied, at his own expense, all the implements, tools and machinery necessary. And in instances, where the parents were destitute, he paid for the children's clothing ; and to the deserving weekly distributed money prizes, besides allowing fair wages for the work done. In fact, such were his enthusiasm and his liberality in the cause, that the recipients of his generous bounties were under the impression that not from his own funds was he dispensing these liberal gifts, but was acting simply as the agent of the government. This benefactor of his race died in 1844, at the ripe old age of ninety-one, respected and venerated by all.

In 1821 McGill University received its charter, and to it many of our best scholars are indebted for their education. In 1852 was incorporated the University of Laval, which has been the *alma mater* of almost all the French-Canadians of note from that time. Mr. Chauveau replaced

Dr. Meilleur as Superintendent of Education in 1855, and introduced many reforms which contributed to the progress of education. He quotes from his official reports and describes the advantages of the adoption of his proposals. In every portion of his department he was indefatigable in abolishing abuses and furthering the cause so dear to him. The educational institutions are divided into five grand classes: 1st, Universities; 2d, Secondary Schools; 3rd, Normal Schools; 4th, Special Schools, and 5th, Primary Schools. A description of these divisions and vast important statistical information are here given. The systems of education followed in New Brunswick, Nova Scotia, Prince Edward Island, Newfoundland, Manitoba and British Columbia are consecutively and succinctly described, with accurate statistical tables. In concluding this chapter, the author gives a comprehensive recapitulation of what has been so fully investigated.

In Chapter XI., Mr. Chauveau, under the heading, "*Mouvement littéraire et intellectuel,*" gives a most interesting digest of the state of literature in Canada, commencing with the publication of newspapers, magazines and scientific journals. He lightly sketches the different works of importance in all the branches of literature which have appeared in the Dominion; this is invaluable to the *littérateur*, supplying at a glance the names of most of the books published in this country, and the names of their authors, carefully classified. In it are also noticed the

" Literary and Historical Society of Quebec," the " Institut Canadien " and other similar societies. The book closes with the reproduction of a lecture upon " Public Education in Canada," delivered by the author at the Canadian Convention in 1874, in Montreal, and forms a brilliant retrospect of Canadian literature.

This work has extended abroad the fame of its author considerably more than any other of his writings, although several of them entitle him to the highest rank as a writer, possessing clearness of thought, conciseness of expression and soundness of judgment.

Mr. Chauveau may be considered as the *doyen* of French-Canadian *littérateurs*. He made his *début* whilst still a very young man, and has ever since faithfully and diligently worked in the same field. One of his earliest productions was " Charles Guérin," which is an intellectual novel, treating of the social habits and customs of the first half of this century. It had a few detractors, but many admirers; none more readily admitted its faults than the author himself—faults of all young writers. The speech made by him in 1855, on the occasion of the inauguration of *Le Monument des Braves* on the Ste. Foye road, on the centenary of the battle of Ste. Foye, and commemorative of that day, was a model of oratory, entitling him to the first rank as a distinguished orator. This high standing he also enjoys in both languages; his discourses are more classical than political,—not by any means a fault, however. The poetical effusions of this gentleman are numerous and bear the evidence of inspiration from the best sources.

J. C. TACHÉ.

This well known gentleman is one of the pioneers of French-Canadian literature, forming with M. M. Quesnel, Bibaud, Parent, Garneau, Laberge, Lenoir and Chauveau, a galaxy of Canadian talent of which any country might well be proud. Mr. Taché made his mark as a journalist many years ago, being a vigorous and hard-hitting opponent, whom his adversaries had often good cause to remember. He has rendered no little service to the public in a number of interesting and clever reports upon important subjects.

In *Trois légendes de mon pays*, are grouped three legends of old Canada, which, the author states, in his prologue, constitute the three parts of a moral drama—similar to the Greek trilogies—symbolizing the religious and social history of the aborigines of the country. In the first, the natives are represented with all their ferocious instincts and in a state of barbarism, before the arrival of the missionaries;—Christianity unknown. In the second, is detailed the conflict of conscience in these wild children of the forest, as they are taught the Word of God;—Christianity preached. And in the third, the final struggle of conscience, followed by the supremacy of religion;—

Christianity triumphant. In other words, here are three legends illustrative of the different phases of mind the savages experienced.

The first, *L'Ilet au massacre, ou l'Evangile ignoré*, opens with the picture of a Micmac encampment on the shores of the Bay of Bic, which is suddenly alarmed by the news that a strong war party of Iroquois was marching against it. A council of chiefs meets, and immediately the old and helpless are sent off to a place of safety down the river. The Micmacs detail two small parties, one to follow the Iroquois and to notify the village of the approach of the enemy, the other to harass them, while the remainder, with their wives and children, seek the shelter of a cave on the island. The first party finds a number of Iroquois canoes and a *cache* of provisions; two of them then leave for the River St. John, to secure the aid of the Malechite tribe, who promptly accede to their request. The Iroquois by this time make their way to the Indian encampment, surround and find it deserted; they, however, next day discover the retreat of the Micmacs on the island and attack them; two assaults are successfully repulsed by the besieged, who are aided by the in-coming tide overflowing the sands and compelling the retreat of the enemy. But a third attack succeeds, and the Micmacs are all massacred. The victorious Iroquois then turn their faces homewards, and divide into two parties, one in search of their canoes and *cache* of provisions, the other to follow more slowly with the wounded. Of the first a number are slain by the relieving party of Malechites, who had come to the assistance of the Micmacs and waited in ambush near the canoes. On the return of the vanquished Iroquois to their camp, they find that all their wounded, twenty in number, had been slaughtered, leaving but fifty warriors of the original hundred, twelve of whom, unable to move from their wounds are despatched to prevent their falling into the hands of their enemies, and their scalps burnt, rather than hang as trophies at the belts of their foes. Again are the Iroquois attacked and lose eleven more men, when the remainder are hunted down and all but five killed, two of whom are claimed as prisoners by the Micmacs and three by the Malechites. The first two are taken to the island, where the Micmacs had been massacred, and are there tortured with the most fiendish cruelty and finally burnt at the stake. The other three are taken to the Malechite encampment on the Madaouaska. The author concludes: It is thus the aborigines acted towards each other before Christianity had been made known to them;—Christianity unknown.

The second legend, *Le Sagamo du Kapskouk ou L'Evangile prêchée*, depicts the missionary labors of *Le Père Masse* among the Malechite Indians, on the River St. John. With intense interest the Indians listen to the development of the Christian doctrines, but when the missionary preaches the forgiveness of enemies, *Le Sagamo* turns a deaf ear, for he has sworn an eternal enmity to the Iroquois. He tells the priest how, when his tribe wished to follow the war-path against the Iroquois, his father's two sons refused to take up the hatchet and were expelled the camp. In despair they joined their natural enemy in company of an Iroquois prisoner, who had been adopted by the Malechites. The following year a large war party of Iroquois, led by the two brothers, descended the River St. John to attack the Malechite village. It was night when they were silently paddling down the river; suddenly, as they neared the Falls of Kapskouk, the war-whoop sounded from two men, standing upright in the foremost canoe, and, as if by enchantment the river shores were lit up by innumerable flambeaux, illuminating and casting a ghastly glare over a most tragic scene; nigh two hundred warriors swept to destruction over the foaming cataract. To obtain this satisfaction the old warrior had been willing to sacrifice the lives of his two sons, for it gave him the melancholy pleasure of boasting to his tribe that "*Mes fils sont des hommes.*" And Sagamo adds: "My father made me swear on his death-bed that I would ever be the bitter enemy of the Iroquois, and to transmit this hatred to my children. How then can you ask me to love my enemies?" But the good priest still perseveres in his mission and in preaching the gospel of truth and love. The precious seed was sown and it required but the generous rain and the rays of the sun to bring forth a rich harvest;—Christianity preached.

The third legend, *Le géant des Méchins, ou L'Evangile acceptée*, is the sudden conversion of an Indian through terror of *Outikou*, the great eater of men, who had been seen by him, and whose apparition was supposed to be followed by fatal results. *Outikou* is exorcised by a missionary and forced to leave his favorite locality near the *Ile aux Méchins*, and his ôui'·n transformed into a cross. The pagan Indian then willingly receives the sacrament of baptism, and his mind is set at rest;—Christianity triumphant.

This volume reflects upon its author credit for his learning, good literary taste and lively imagination. These three legends are written with much art, breathing a spirit of poetry and religious enthusiasm, and the diction employed is remarkable for purity and elegance. Any desirous of further studying the style of this author can not do better than read his best effort: *Forestiers et Voyageurs*.

J. M. LeMOINE.

Among Canadian writers, no name is better known in English circles than that of Mr. LeMoine, and there can be no doubt that his patriotic labors greatly contributed to making the Dominion more fully known both at home and abroad, and to exciting a deep interest in its past records, institutions and history. With a diligence and public spirit, rare in any community, this gentleman has devoted himself—and no weaker word than *devoted* would convey the full sense of his untiring labors and researches in the work of discovery—to publishing the most valuable archives of the country, dating from the foundation of the colony and illustrating these memorials with remarks upon its topography and histoty; in fact, carefully accumulating a mass of useful, historical and legendary materials, to which French, English, American and Canadian writers have frequently confessed their indebtedness. He has had the good fortune to gain access to private manuscripts and journals of the oldest families, and these have considerably aided him in disentangling those portions of history hitherto involved in the mazes of doubt and uncertainty. Every event, ancient, or recent, awakening the interest or exciting the patriotism of the public, has been carefully canvassed and sifted ; his writings throughout, in tone, sentiment and fact exhibit a genuine love of country and a pride in the transactions of her eminent men, from its first settlement to the present day. The reading community cheerfully acknowledge their gratitude to his valuable and voluntary literary services; in the preparation of *Old and New Canada* in which I have been engaged since last year, I have had several occasions of referring to this gentleman's works and I may add with gratifying results each time.

Quebec, Past and Present, a History of Quebec, with illustrations, by the above gentleman, is divided into two parts; the first treats of the history of the colony from 1608 to 1875 ; and the second comprises a description of the city of the present day.

In the introduction, the author gives a rapid sketch of the discovery of Canada, Jacques Cartier's landing at Stadacona (1535), and his subsequent voyages. The intrepid mariner of St. Malo and his men passed their first winter on the banks of the St. Charles, where they underwent untold sufferings from want of provisions, cold and scurvy. All but three or four were attacked by this distressing disease, and were cured only through the advice of an Indian to use a decoction of spruce. In the spring of the following year, Jacques Cartier returned to France, and again visited Canada in 1541, when he sailed up the St. Lawrence and explored the rapids above Hochelaga, in the hope of finding a passage to China. In the autumn, discouraged and despairing, he left the colony, in spite of the wishes of Roberval, whom he met in the Gulf, and who continued his voyage to Quebec and made his winter-quarters at Cap Rouge. It was only by strict discipline an harsh measures, that he succeeded in keeping the members of his party together, and shortly afterwards he returned to Europe. Mr. LeMoine adds : " Canadian annals from 1542 to 1608 offer a perfect blank, no Europeans having remained behind."

The work proper begins with a fanciful description of the laying of the foundation of the settlement of Quebec by Champlain in 1608. On the site of the present church of *Notre Dame des Victoires*, in the Lower Town, he erected a *habitation*, and storehouses, of which a woodcut is given, and, although without perspective, or proportion, conveys a good idea of this group of buildings. Later, barracks were built for the soldiery in the Upper Town, in the vicinity of the *Place d'armes*. Shortly afterwards, Champlain believed himself obliged to take sides with the Hurons against the Iroquois, a powerful combination of five nations, whose warlike character, ferocious disposition and atrocious cruelties were a terror to all other tribes. This led to fierce wars which lasted over a century, and ended in the almost complete annihilation of the Algonquin and Huron nations. It would be difficult to compute the myriads of lives that fell victims to their reeking tomahawks and bloody scalping knives. In 1615, the Recollet Fathers arrived in Quebec, and in 1619 they founded a monastery on the banks of the St. Charles, where now stands the General Hospital. In 1617 and 1618 a famine raged amongst the colonists and scurvy thinned their ranks to an alarming extent. Champlain brought out to Quebec, two years later, a young and beautiful bride, on which occasion there was great rejoicing in the city, but the rigors of the climate, the constant dread of Indian attacks and the hardships of a colonial life were too much for one of her delicate frame, and soon she returned to France. During her short stay her winning and graceful manners endeared her to all. In 1629, Champlain was obliged, through stress of circumstances, to deliver up the fortress of Quebec to the Kirke brothers, who were bearers of Letters of Marque from the King of England. Quebec was, however, by the Saint Germain Treaty of 1632, restored to France, and Champlain returned to the colony in 1633, accompanied by the Jesuit Fathers, Massé and Brebœuf, and in this year, in performance of a vow, he erected a church to *Notre Dame de Recouvrance* on the eastern portion of the site of the present Basilica. This latter was commenced in 1647. On Christmas day, 1635, Champlain died after two months' illness, at the age of sixty-eight. In 1637, the Jesuits' College was constructed, and rebuilt in 1720 on a much more extensive scale; known to the present generation as the lately demolished Jesuits' barracks. In 1639, the *Ursuline* and *Hospitalières* nuns reached Quebec; the former, accompanied by Madame de la Peltrie, who founded the *Ursuline* Convent, for the purpose of instructing the Indian children, and eventually those of the colonists; the latter ladies to undertake the care of the sick, and to that end, assisted thereto by the generous liberality of the Duchess d'Aiguillon, established the *Hôtel-Dieu*. The history of both these institutions is given at length; the good they have effected and the importance, which they have attained, have been recognized by all denominations from those early times to the present, and are enthusiastically dwelt upon in this volume. In 1649, the Jesuit missionaries—Fathers Gabriel Lallemant and de Breboeuf, after enduring inconceivable tortures, were cruelly murdered by the Iroquois, near Lake Simcoe. In 1659, Monseigneur de Laval landed at Quebec as its first Bishop. A description of the earthquake of 1663 is given, and of the extraordinary celestial phenomena attending it. It is related to have been felt at intervals for nearly six months, during which, three distinct suns were visible; "the true sun in the centre, and the reflected ones on either side." The same optical illusion occurred seven days later and a total eclipse of the sun shortly afterwards; during that time the earth was violently convulsed. In the same year, Quebec was granted a Royal Government, and an extensive system of fortification was inaugurated, under the able administration of the Count de Frontenac, with whom were sent out several companies of the famous Carignan regiment. These immediately commenced the construction of forts in different parts of the country, preparatory to taking the offensive against the Iroquois, who had hitherto carried war into the heart of the colony, but had been left unmolested in their own *châteaux-forts*. On the 4th February, 1667, the first "ball" in Canada was given at the Château St. Louis and theatrical performances were acted,—not only there, but within the walls of the Ursulines and Hôtel-Dieu, to the great scandal of many, especially Bishop Laval. But the Count de Frontenac was a firm ruler and all had to bow to his mandates, be he priest or layman. Mr. LeMoine gives interesting details of the habits and customs of these days, which will be agreeable reading to many. The Intendant's Palace, a full description of which is furnished, fell a prey to the flames in 1713, but was rebuilt on a grander scale by the Intendant Begon at the expense of the French King. After the cession it fell into decay, was occupied by the American troops in 1775, during the winter of the blockade, and was finally destroyed by the bombardment from the city. The dreadful "Lachine massacre" occurred in 1689, creating the greatest dismay among the colonists and rousing them to reprisals against the supposed instigators. Then were planned the New England campaigns, which proved so disastrous to the Anglo-Saxon colonists. This, of course, led to retaliations, and expeditions by land and water were organized to avenge the disasters of Schenectady and Salmon Falls. The land force, under Winthrop and Schuyler, proved a perfect failure ; while the fleet, under Sir William Phipps, attempted an ineffectual bombardment of Quebec. The Admiral essayed a land attack with no better results, and he returned discomfited to Boston. It was on this occasion that Frontenac delivered his famous and dauntless reply to the English envoy. From England, in 1711, was sent Sir Hovenden Walker with a large fleet to secure the conquest of Canada ; but the expedition ended most disastrously. Several frigates, with their crews, marines and soldiers, were wrecked and hopelessly lost on Egg Island, obliging the return of the Admiral to England. A thrilling word-painting of this awful catastrophe from *Les Promenades du Golfe*, by Mr. Faucher, is given and will be reviewed in this volume. For the deliverance from these two imminent dangers, the little chapel in the Lower Town was dedicated to *Notre Dame des Victoires*. The *Château St. Louis* and the gay times, which made merry its sombre walls, are next related. As an interesting relic of the old past, are described the proceedings followed in the ceremony of a vassal rendering "faith and homage" to his seignior, and also those of a seignior to his sovereign. In

1748, the infamous Bigot arrived as Intendant of New France. Mr. LeMoine dilates upon the execrable acts of this worthy, and to him he ascribes all the miseries and misfortunes which soon overtook the colony.* A dire famine weighed heavily upon it in 1755, but this merely gave to the unscrupulous Bigot opportunities of making profits out of the provisions, sent by the French King to his famishing subjects. He established a store in connection with his Palace and vended these provisions at exorbitant prices to the starving poor: hence was derived the name of *La Friponne*. Mr. LeMoine states that as many as three hundred died from inanition and its consequent miseries; and that these wretched beings were to be seen staggering about the streets of Quebec the whole day long, vainly imploring aid. In the midst of all this poverty and distress, Bigot held high revelry and was surrounded by courtezans and sycophants, who rioted in luxury and vice at the public expense. His extravagant follies vied with even the wild recklessness and lavishness of the French court. But this heartless profligacy was soon to end; and great was the excitement on both sides of the St. Lawrence and in the capital, when in the spring of 1759 an English fleet proudly sailed up the river. Old and young gallantly volunteered for the defence of their "hearths and homes," and a general enthusiasm

---

*This, methinks, a somewhat overdrawn statement, for there were many other causes operating to bring about the final overthrow of French power.

prevailed among "seignior and vassal." Rapid preparations were made for the coming struggle; weak places in the fortifications were strengthened and new lines of earthworks raised. The men-of-war, frigates and sloops of the English fleet, with their numerous transports, made an imposing sight in the grand harbor of Quebec. On the night of the 28th June there was an attempt to fire this fleet, which was anchored near the Island of Orleans, by launching, during the ebb-tide, fire ships and rafts charged with deadly fire-works, grenades and other combustibles, which, as they approached the vessels, sent up their lurid flames into the sombre night, casting reflections on the clear surface of the river and producing the grandest spectacle imaginable, but entirely failing of injuring the fleet. The battle of Beauport, on the 31st of July, so disastrous to the army of Wolfe, is fully described; as also that of the Plains of Abraham, 13th September, with the death of both generals on its blood-stained field. On the 18th Quebec capitulated, and the red cross of England replaced the *fleur-de-lis* on the citadel. A sorry sight the city presented after the seige; there was hardly a building left standing which was not riddled through. Famine, scurvy and other diseases created great ravages during the following winter, especially among the soldiery, nearly one-half of whom died. The French, under de Lévis, with a fairly disciplined and strong force, reappeared before the city on the 28th of April following, when Murray rashly led out his troops, engaged the enemy at Ste. Foye and was defeated. At this battle the loss was four thousand men (?) on both sides, and had the French acted with promptness, the city might have been easily retaken. The arrival of an English fleet shortly afterwards caused the French army to retreat with precipitation, abandoning all their camp equipage and war material. With the subsequent surrender of Montreal, on the 8th of September, 1760, terminated the French *régime* in Canada.

Shortly after the inauguration of British rule, the *Quebec Gazette* appeared in French and English. The " new subjects " soon became reconciled to the changed order of things and matters went on smoothly in the colony until the passage of the *Quebec Act*, in 1774, which created discontent among the British. The seige and blockade of the city by Montgomery and Arnold, in 1775, are minutely detailed, and the chivalrous conduct of General Carleton is highly lauded. A well merited tribute is paid to the loyalty of both French and English, who honorably resisted the blandishments and seductions held out to them by the American rebels. The phenomena of the " two dark Sundays," the 9th and 16th October, 1785, are mentioned, and to meteorologists will be interesting. Admiral Nelson's love affair with a daughter of Quebec, when captain of H.M.S. " Albermale," and the rough method adopted by his brother officers to end a romantic affair are recounted. In 1791, H.R.H. Prince Edward, visited Quebec, and a public reception was given him ; that same year Canada was divided into two provinces by proclamation, and the same year the first parliament was held in Quebec, The revolutionary events in France in 1793 painfully affected the residents of Quebec, and Lord Dorchester issued a proclamation against the emissaries of anarchy. Upon this plea, says the author, on several occasions later on, the French Canadians were needlessly and purposely oppressed. A description of a visit to Quebec, towards the end of last century, of the Micmacs, numbering four hundred, in full war-paint and costumes, and their antics is a graphic recital. In 1804, the English Cathedral was erected upon the site of the church and monastery of the *Frères Recollets*, which were consumed by fire on the 6th September, 1796. The first trial for high treason, under British rule, was that of David McLane, in 1797, who was condemned and put to death in a barbarously cruel manner, in obedience to the draconic law of that period. The tyrannical operations of press gangs are noted. Towards the end of last century, slavery was still in existence here, but was finally abolished in 1803. Steam navigation was first accomplished between Quebec and Montreal, on the 6th November, 1809, the passage occupying sixty-six hours. In March, 1810, *Le Canadien* was suppressed for publishing libellous articles on the policy of Sir James Craig, the then Governor-General ; and a short time afterwards M. M. Bédard, Taschereau and Blanchet were arrested on charges of sedition. There are furnished short sketches of the war of 1812, between England and the United States, with the alternate successes and defeats of either side. Among the incidents of that war is mentioned the arrival in Quebec, as a prisoner, of General Winfield Scott, who afterwards distinguished himself in Mexico. In 1824, " The Literary and Historical Society of Quebec " was founded by the Earl of Dalhousie. In 1827, was erected the monument in the Governor's garden, to the memory of Wolfe and Montcalm, a description of which is supplied. In 1832, the first ocean steamer, the " Royal William," built at Quebec, sailed from this port to cross the Atlantic. The dreadful scenes, during the cholera of 1832, are depicted in all their ghastliness, and details of its subsequent visitations of 1834, 1849, 1851, 1852 and 1854 are also given. The numerous acts of robbery and violence, committed by the Chambers' gang and the wide-spread terror existing in consequence, and their final arrest and punishment are noticed. Of the revolution of 1837 Mr. LeMoine makes but slight mention. He, however, treats this subject at length, in his " Maple Leaves." Lord Durham's rule is alluded to in flattering terms; and he is praised as one of the truest friends Canada has ever known. Then follows a series of sad and heart-rending misfortunes. The " fall of the rock " in Champlain street, in 1841, crushing many houses and their inmates : the fires of St. Roch and St.

John suburbs, in 1845, rendering thousands homeless and causing more than forty human beings to perish in the flames: the burning of the theatre near Durham Terrace, when nearly fifty people met an appalling death : the fever epidemic among the emigrants in 1847, when hundreds fell victims to this dreadful disease, and myriads of orphans were thrown upon the mercy and charity of the world : and the frightful loss of the steamer " Montreal," and a portion of its living freight, by fire, in 1857. These are all events conjuring up hosts of trying memories to most Quebecers. On the other hand, as gleams of sunshine to relieve the above sad pictures, are the formation of a line of steamships between England and Quebec, and the opening of the Grand Trunk Railway ; both of which enterprises have materially contributed to the prosperity of Canada. The Ste. Foye monument " to the braves of 1760" was inaugurated in 1863, with great *éclat* and ceremony ; the monument and neighboring scenery are graphically portrayed. In 1864, the military laboratory in the Artillery Park exploded and several soldiers lost their lives; while in 1866, St. Roch was again reduced to ashes, when Lieutenant Baine, of the Royal Artillery, met his death in chivalrous and praiseworthy endeavors to save life and property. The English troops evacuated the city in 1871, and the citadel and other fortifications were handed over to the Dominion Government. In 1872, Lord Dufferin arrived as Governor-General ; his fame, as a statesman and a *littérateur*, had preceded him, and it was with genuine satisfaction he was greeted upon his arrival. It is no exaggeration to state that he was the most popular governor who has ruled Canada, not only in his official character, but in his private capacity. He sailed from these shores, bearing with him the regrets of all, and leaving behind the most pleasing memories of his intellectual abllities and social qualities; his admired countess was equally popular throughout. In 1867, the era of confederation was inaugurated, which has so completely altered the political condition of the different provinces, and formed out of a number of petty, divided states, a powerful and wealthy Dominion, which even now classes as fourth in the list of maritime nations. In the same year, the remains of the historian Garneau were translated to Belmont Cemetery, accompanied by a vast concourse of friends and admirers, and, on this occasion, the Hon. P. J. O. Chauveau delivered one of his master-pieces of oratory, worthy of the great man whose memory he was honoring. The proceedings of the Laval bi-centenary are faithfully and interestingly detailed. The chapter then closes with a description of the theatrical representation, at the citadel, of the scene enacted on December 31st, 1775, when Montgomery made his unsuccessful attack upon Quebec. Mr. LeMoine reproduces an article of "The Chronicle," "upon the plans of

improvement of the City of Quebec, suggested by Lord
Dufferin, with designs of the new castle of St. Louis, and
the different gates" to be constructed.

In the second part of this work are given full
descriptions of the citadel and fortifications, the walls, gates
and the forts of Levis, with views of the ancient gates, and
also valuable information respecting the different institutions and buildings of the city.

In dedicating " Quebec Past and Present" to our citizens, Mr. LeMoine presented them with a valuable
work, replete with information unknown to many of them,
and he richly deserves thanks for his untiring zeal and research in collecting the material for such a book. To the
tourist and general traveler it will be a *sine quâ non*, and
as necessary as their satchel and traveling rug. It will
supply them, while in the city, with the details they need
in reference to the different localities and their history, and
with interesting reading matter, which will not be soon forgotten. This work evinces study of points of history
and topography of the regions traversed by the author;
the lights and shadows of life are agreeably presented and
interwoven with historical facts and local traditions.

With regard to Mr. LeMoine's style, a few ungenerous
comments have, at times, been made, but, as he says in
his preface " It is less fine writing and elaborate sentences
I aim at than a familiar narrative." It must be remembered that he writes in two languages, and is necessarily

limited as to time, while often composing under the influence of that natural zeal which urges an early publication of valuable information, regardless of merely literary ornament One of the striking characteristics of the works of this author is the enthusiasm with which he narrates facts. The animating principle guiding him deserves the highest respect of the community, for it is simple patriotism and a commendable desire to preserve and illustrate the glorious annals of our country. His books might justly be called *répertoires* of the valuable historical data of the primitive experiences and most important events of the old French colony down to the time of the Cession, and thence to our own day. The value of such writings can not be overestimated; in fact they are of a public character, and should be cherished and prized by every private citizen and lover of his country.

L'ABBÉ R. H. CASGRAIN.

The anecdotes and legends of our old Canadian history must ever prove attractive and fascinating, not only to the patriotic reader, but to every one capable of appreciating the elements of lofty sentiment and stirring romance. In this valuable historic domain much excellent work has been performed by L'Abbé Casgrain and other writers, whose books will be noticed in these reviews, and in it yet remain materials of the most useful kind, for the uprearing hereafter of many a fair fabric of history and fancy. None of the laborers in this department has worked to better advantage so far, or gained more credit than the Abbé. Employing language happily suited to his subject and animated by the romantic and chivalric spirit of the age he treats of, he depicts with sympathy and admiration some of the most moving events of the olden time,—deadly combats with the aborigines, incidents of their savage warfare, tortures of captured enemies, perilous adventures of all kinds, arduous struggles of the hardy pioneers against the most varied difficulties and misfortunes, beauties of Canadian scenery at every change of season and prospect, multiform and most vigorous passions,—everything in fact which goes to make that world within and that larger universe without, which have been the mysteries of ages, as perplexing and insoluble as when, three thousand years ago the sages of ancient Greece strove with sharpened intellects and profound insight to reveal its attractive yet evasive secrets. I may mention, at the outset, that the Abbé states that the legends and anecdotes he recounts are not mere creations of the imagination, but authentically substantiated, which, doubtless, will render these narratives still more interesting to the reader.

Les Opuscules by the Abbé is divided into two parts: Firstly, *Les Pionniers Canadiens*, in which is given the dark side of Indian life ; the murder of a white man and his wife and the abduction of the latter's sister, whose fate is never ascertained. The tale involves the dastardly slaughter of a young officer and the subsequent miserable death of the murderer from the bite of a snake—his loathsome corpse repelling all beholders. In harrowing phrase, the writer describes the murderer's attempt to force a lady, who had been a witness of his crime, to drink of the dead man's blood, and the consequences of the fiendish act. The story is effectively told and is worthy of perusal, if for nothing else than the light it sheds upon early Canadian life. The author believes that it is the perpetration of such crimes, which have brought upon the Indians the maledictions which hang over them to this day, resulting in their gradual extinction.

Secondly, *Un pèlèrinage à l'Isle aux Coudres*, which is a graphic pen and ink description of the Island, its principal souvenirs, historical and legendary, with faithful delineations of the customs, habits and occupations of its inhabitants. Jacques Cartier landed here and heard the first mass celebrated in Canada—7th September, 1535. The English fleet, under Wolfe, anchored opposite it, and the grandson of Admiral Durell was taken prisoner while ashore shooting and brought to Quebec. The wreck of two vessels "The Rosalind" and "John Balckfoot" in 1832 is related, and the kind treatment of the officers and men, during the winter they passed on the island, exhibits the hearty and hospitable nature of its primitive people. A delightful and absorbing account follows of the Arcadian life of the first settlers, and of the happiness and innocence of the children. The book closes with the tradition of the death of the *Rev. Père de la Brosse* in 1782, at Tadousac, at the age of sixty-eight. He was hale and hearty and sitting at a game of cards with a few friends, when he suddenly informed them that he should die that night at twelve o'clock, and that his death should be proclaimed to them by the tolling of the church bell. They were incredulous, but at midnight, hearing the predicted ominous sounds, his friends ran to the church and there found the venerable priest, prostrate before the altar, cold in death. At the same moment, the church bells of the different parishes, in which he had officiated at one time or another, rang loudly; and the Rev. M. Compain, then curé on the island, was informed by a solemn voice of the death of the rev. father, and that a canoe would meet him at the end of the island and convey him to Tadousac to perform the funeral rites of the deceased. *Père de la Brosse* had also given instructions the evening of his demise to send for the Rev. M. Compain, who, he said, would be ready to accompany the party sent in search of him. In 1846, a living witness testified to the truth of these facts.

The original settlers of the island must have possessed wonderful appetites if M. François Tremblay's version be correct. Perhaps it may be pleasing to give an account of an entertainment in those days, the costumes worn by the guests, and the bill of fare. I therefore quote M. Tremblay: " Imagine," he asks you, " thirty or forty good eaters, of those times, at table.. There was little ceremony, but everything was offered in the heartiest manner and each took the place he could find. Chairs were not in common use; on each side of the table were blocks of wood on which boards were placed, and trunks here and there were used as seats; the guests not thus accommodated, standing. On the table were leaden or common delf dishes, and if there were enough for all it was an indication of wealth. The few forks were reserved for the women and each provided his own knife. The clothing of the men consisted of grey home-spun pants of country cloth and a pair of *bottes sauvages;* and the *bonnets bleus,* generally worn out-of-doors, were laid aside. Their toilette was completed by a dicky, without which—dreadful to relate—they were not entitled to partake of pie, a favorite dish of the *habitant.* The costumes of the women consisted of a blue skirt with white stripes, and a flowered Indian shawl and a white cap completed their attire on gala days. The preparations for a festival were something formidable, if one is to judge from what follows, and recall the feast of Gargantua. In the first place was prepared a *ragoût* of pork, beef, or mutton, in a thirty or forty gallon boiler; minced *pâtés,* large pies, pork chops, *apprêtés* in a variety of ways; quarters of veal, mutton, fowl and game. Besides the viands, there were pastries of different kinds, cooked in lard or porpoise oil, and cakes now known as *croquignoles.* All these were simultaneously placed on the table, and each helped himself as he pleased. Those who had no plate took a piece of pastry from a *pâté* and used it as a dish. Politeness required that each should see that his neighbor lacked nothing. When it was noticed that the supply of food was becoming short before any one, he was addressed as follows, " Brother, you excite pity," and was immediately provided with more. Whilst the eatables were being partaken of, the host went round the table and poured out a glass of liquor to each in a cup or pewter goblet. The utmost gaiety prevailed; hunting and fishing exploits were recounted and the feast ended with songs, the choruses of which were joined in by the whole company." This narrative is quaintly told and has to be perused in the language of the author to be thoroughly enjoyed.

A rather amusing incident, which might have been followed by tragic results, is given; some men in an open boat are overtaken by a storm and in imminent danger of being drowned; one is praying very fervently, when suddenly a heavier gust of wind nearly upsets the boat, which calls from him the following comical though touching appeal: "Oh, God! if you mean to do anything, do it quickly; were we at the bottom it would be too late; how could you allow us to perish? my poor old mother, my wife and children are still dependent upon and require me;" and he continues, "*allons, mon Dieu, encore un petit coup de coeur, j'allons échapper.*" It is just such episodes that give the student a correct insight into traits and characteristics of a people.

The captivating style of the Abbé is further manifested in *Les Légendes Canadiennes*, which first appeared in *Les Soirées Canadiennes*. One can not lay down this book unfinished without feeling an eager desire to read it through, for, by soul-stirring legends and stories, the writer rivets one's attention, and fills him with a sense of the reality and picturesque character of his tales. It was only the other day that a friend of mine, a distinguished *littéra-*

teur, reminded me how anxiously we had looked forward to each number of *Les Soirées Canadiennes*, containing the work under review, and the effect its perusal had in exciting our imagination, and charming away many hours. "For my own part," he added, "the reading of these *Légendes* and that of *Les Anciens Canadiens* first created in me a taste for a literary career." Many more have doubtless derived inspiration from the same sources.

The first legend is, *Le tableau de la Rivière Ouelle*, one of the earliest productions of the Abbé, and which abundantly exhibits the spirit of exuberant youth, delighting in thrilling events and striking colors. But this natural effervescence allowed for, the book, in matter and style, maintains a decided interest throughout. Of a stormy, blustry winter evening, at Rivière Ouelle, a mother, with her little folk around her, narrates to please them the following tradition: Towards the middle of last century, a father and son, officers of the French army, attended by a soldier and an Indian guide, are tramping through the forest on the south shore of the St. Lawrence. The guide is killed by an Indian of another tribe, who, in his turn, is shot by the younger officer. The remaining three proceed on their way, but, as might be expected, soon lose themselves, become exhausted from fatigue and hunger, and the father and soldier succumb to their fate, while the survivor falls into a sort of trance, in which, arrayed in her heavenly splendor and surrounded by clouds of glory and bright visions, the Blessed Virgin appears to him and promises aid. He awakes to find coming towards him a Jesuit father who carries him to a *habitant* house ; a genuine description of which is given ;—a faithful counterpart of the dwellings of the present day. This picture of a rural dwelling has been greatly admired for its quaintness and truthfulness and has often been reproduced by many eminent French writers. The young officer afterwards presents a painting to the chapel in the vicinity, now the old church of Rivière Ouelle. This *Tableau* to be appreciated in its varied features has to be read in its entirety.

The next tale in this volume is *La Jongleuse*. It opens in the City of Quebec, in the olden time. On a dark night, Madame Houel, attended by a *coureur de bois* named *Le Canotier*, and an Indian, *Grande Couleuvre*, is leaving the city with her son, a lad between eight and ten years of age, in a bark canoe, to join her husband, some ninety miles down the river. The boy, shortly after their departure, has a vision,—a white woman who scowls threateningly and terrifies him. It is the apparition of *Le Jongleuse*, a sort of Indian witch, who, it is said, with fiendish cruelty inflicts more agony than the severest tortures of the redskins. Her appearance is but the forerunner of evil, for they are soon attacked by the Iroquois and nearly captured. They succeed in escaping through a clever stratagem of *Le Canotier*, who, favored by the darkness, noiselessly slips into the water, swims towards the Indians, seven in number, and upsets their canoe. Madame Houel and her party escape and go ashore to camp for the rest of the night. The following day, in the absence of *Le Canotier*, the Indian is killed and scalped, but not before he had slain two of the attacking party ; and Madame Houel and her son are carried off as prisoners. When *Le Canotier* returns, he is stricken with grief at the sight of the corpse of the friend he had loved so well, and who had been his companion for many years in the chase and in the field. He mournfully fulfills the last offices, and plants over his grave a wooden cross, in the centre of which he transfixes with the knife of *Grande Couleuvre* the scalps of the two dead Indians. "*Etrange et terrible trophée, mais digne de ce héros des bois.*"

Many years have elapsed, and young Houel, now grown to manhood, returns with *Le Canotier* to the vicinity of *La Rivière Ouelle* to recover the remains of his mother and transport them to France. The sequel of the above tragic events is continued. The Iroquois who had captured young Houel and his mother take them down the river in canoes. In a few days afterwards, at the instigation of *La Jongleuse*, the death tortures are prepared. After much preliminary and ingenious cruelty, an Indian climbs a tree and bends down a large branch, to the end of which he attaches two long leather thongs, one of which is wound around the trunk of a tree, whilst the bough is still bent and one end placed in the hands of the boy

and the other tied around the neck of his unfortunate
mother. The ordeal is a terrible one, for were his
strength to give way he should become the executioner
of his mother. The critical position is realized by
both; he receives her blessings and last adieux. Over-
come by fatigue and exhausted by intense excitement,
nature gives way and he temporarily loses consciousness. In terror, he awakes to find the thong slipping
through his benumbed fingers and to hear its grating
sound on the bark of the tree. With a desperate effort
he renews his grasp, but he succumbs and again swoons.
On regaining his senses later on, he beholds the corpse of his
beloved mother pitilessly swinging in the air. Such refin-
ement of cruelty can hardly be conceived and the effect was
frightful on the mind of the poor boy who was ever afterwards haunted by the ghastly spectacle. Nothing in pathos
can exceed the description of the death of Madame Houel
at the unwilling hands of her helpless son, her heartrend-
ing appeals, her martyr-like resignation and her prayers
for her inhuman executioners.

Le Canotier then takes up the thread of the story:
After having repaired the canoe, which the Iroquois had
cut in several places, he starts in pursuit and reaches
their vicinity a few days later. He finds them eight in
number holding an orgie with *La Jongleuse;* they had
carelessly left their loaded guns unguarded, which he
secures, and, cautiously creeping up to them, he succeeds

in killing six, when the two remaining rush towards him. He aims at the first but his gun misses fire; nothing daunted, however, he throws his dagger at the Indian with such force that it pierces his heart. The survivor, a man of giant stature and immense strength, closes with him. After a violent struggle *Le Canotier* wrests from the Indian his knife and puts an end to the conflict. Then he vainly searches for *La Jongleuse*, and returns to find the body of Madame Houel suspended to a tree, and the inanimate form of her boy near by, whom, after assiduous care and attendance, he succeeds in bringing back to consciousness. To his horror the boy's hair from a jet black had become white as snow.

On the evening of the recital, M. Houel and *Le Canotier* leave the shore in a canoe, bearing the remains of his unfortunate mother, and were watched with tearful eyes by the kind-hearted *habitant*, till they had rounded the point of *La Rivière Ouelle*. The fate of *La Jongleuse* is unknown, but it is thought to have some relation to the death of an Indian woman, who had the reputation of being a witch, and who, in her last moments, at her own request, was attended by a priest. Thus by a striking dispensation of Providence, the prayer of Madame Houel had found acceptance. Certain writers pretend that the lugubrious wailing sounds heard at Rivière Ouelle, which terrify so many are the lamentations of *La Jongleuse*, who implores the prayers of the just. It will be observed that the Abbé has followed in all his legends the rules he laid down, to give "*d'un coté le tableau historique conservé sur des monuments encore existants—de l'autre, l'image féerique, reflétée dans l'onde populaire.*"

L'Abbé Casgrain is imbued with the spirit of Chateaubriand and Lamartine, especially of the latter. The beauty of his style, its form, the sonorous amplitude of the sentences are deeply characteristic of him. He delights in rounded periods, brilliant words and a rush of sympathetic phrases, whose refrain strikes harmoniously on the ear. Like the possessor of a well-trained vocal organ he is pleased with his own voice; he sings and listens to himself with rapture; but he sings well and pleases others besides himself. The Abbé's works are read with ever increasing interest. His varied knowledge, industry and research are worthy of the highest eulogium. His descriptions are full of the power and intensity of true poetry; and the events and episodes of which he treats stand forth in clear and coherent outline. Dramatic power, vigorous portraiture and artistic construction are other features characterizing his productions. The Abbé has written several other works, but it is generally conceded that his masterpieces are his *Histoire de la Mère Marie de l'Incarnation*, and *L'Histoire de l'Hôtel-Dieu de Québec.* His achievements in poetry are also very creditable, but I can not here write of them.

PROFESSOR HUBERT LaRUE.

All will read with pleasure a work published by a gentleman of the culture of Dr. LaRue, for there can be no doubt that his literary performances excite public attention. It is very much to his honor, that in the intervals of his many occupations, and, during hours by others devoted to amusement and relaxation, he finds time to contribute to the store of Canadian literature.

Mélanges d'histoire, de littérature et d'économie politique, by the learned professor, is a series of essays and sketches evincing much knowledge of life. Under the comprehensive title of *Nos qualités et nos défauts*, he treats of four subjects. The first is, *La Langue Française au Canada*, in which is criticized the French used in this country; the author contending, that the *habitants* have preserved their mother-tongue with greater purity than any other class, and that the expressions employed by them are still in vogue in France, in the different departments from which their ancestors emigrated. Mr. LaRue gives instances of the singularity of some of the expressions and compares them with those found in the earliest writers, proving that they are identical. The language of artizans and laborers, he, however, finds freely intermixed with Anglicisims, which he ascribes to their intercourse with English speaking nationalities. Mr. LaRue taxes advocates and others of the liberal professions with speaking incorrectly, and appeals to them to set a better example; he also exhorts the ladies to use their influence in preventing the use of Anglicisms. This desire, on the part of so well educated a gentleman, to preserve *sa belle langue* in its purity, is praiseworthy and natural. He feelingly alludes to the injustice done French-Canadians by Chateaubriand in his brilliant works on America, in *René, Atala et les Natchez* especially, wherein he represents them as savages, living in a still more savage country. The Professor believes Chateaubriand to be responsible, to a great extent, for the erroneous impressions prevailing in France and elsewhere, concerning this country. In illustration of which he relates seeing a picture in a shop window, at Louvain, having for title "Canadian mothers at their children's graves," which ludicrously excited him, and the description of which must convulse his readers with laughter.

The second paper, *Paresse et Travail*, is a dissertation on the dangers and seductions of idleness, and the reward of labor and perseverance. It is written in choice and correct language, flavored with laconic humor of a distinctive kind.

The third paper, *Luxe et Vanité*, is simply to be considered comparatively, for what might be thought a luxury by one, would be the necessity of another; many things assumed to be luxuries are in reality matters of custom and almost indispensable. In regard to another subject, the author is also right; a certain class of our population spend on their clothing more than their means justify; in fact they often stint themselves at table, in order to indulge in the vanity of·dress. Then follows an eloquent picture of the folly of such action. If these remarks could reach those they are intended for, they might prove very beneficial, as the advice is worthy of serious attention. The present generation of Canadians differ greatly from their ancesters, in this respect, and also from the same classes in France to-day, who are thrifty and economical to a degree, not easily understood by ourselves. The recuperative powers of France, as manifested since the Franco-Prussian war, are undoubtedly due to this commendable practice.

The fourth and last paper, *Notaires Avocats et Medecins*, is a highly humorous sketch of the different professional traits of the members of the liberal professions, showing up their peculiarities and comical aspects. The pictures are not overdrawn, being but too faithful in many instances. Celtic humor pervades this paper, and renders its perusal highly agreeable.

Le défricheur de langue, tragédie bouffe, is a cleverly written parody of an article "hi-falutin" and ludicrous to a degree upon *La langue Française et la Nationalité*, which appeared in a periodical called *La Ruche littéraire*, published in Montreal by an eccentric French refugee, M. H. Emile Chevalier, and another equally amusing on *L'Histoire d'une bonne poésie*, by M. Vogéli. These shafts of ridicule proved the death-blow of the magazine, such keen shafts of wit and satire, made *La Ruche littéraire* the laughing stock of the whole province.

Eloge funèbre de M. L'Abbé Louis-Jacques Casault, the founder and first rector of Laval University, is an able *résumé* of the valuable labors of the deceased, and especially of the great services he rendered that celebrated institution. Mr. LaRue recounts the manifold difficulties that Mr. Casault had to contend with before maturing his project of endowing Canada with a university, that should be second to none in America. It was fitting that he, who had conceived the idea, should have the administration, and from its inauguration, in 1850, to his death, in 1860, it remained under his wise and efficient guidance. Mr. LaRue pays, in an appropriate strain, a high tribute to the energy, ability, erudition and charity of the departed. In grateful terms, he expresses personal indebtedness to valuable kindnesses of which he was the recipient. The great intellectual advantages, accruing to Canada from this institution, are forcibly brought out ; and they certainly can not be overestimated.

Discours de fin d'Année is, as its title indicates, a short valedictory address to the students of Laval University, on the eve of the long vacation, in which is given the history of holidays from the earliest times. The author states that there is no record of any protest on the part of students against *congés*, nor has legislation ever been sought to prevent their recurrence. The directions to the students are wise and thoughtful. But who can ever forget the delight we all have experienced on such occasions? This thought conjures up in my mind the pleasurable emotions of boyhood and excites unavailable regrets that I can never again experience similar happiness.

Un naufrage dans le Golfe St. Laurent, is an exciting narrative of a shipwreck, with all its harrowing details. This story is fairly well told.

Les "Mémoires" de M. de Gaspé. Those, who have read these *Mémoires*, can easily imagine how they would be appreciated by one possessing the tastes of the professor. Mr. LaRue says: "*J'ai lu ce livre tout d'un trait sans m'arrêter un instant.*" This is a great compliment, but it is deserved, for a more pleasing book, it has seldom been my lot to read. The author selects the most telling passages, with which to delight his readers, and to give an idea of the characteristic style of Mr. de Gaspé. One of our distinguished journalists once wrote: "Although Mr. de Gaspé is seventy-six years of age, he is, in spirit, our youngest writer;" and this every one will acknowledge. There can be no doubt that the *Mémoires* are a *chef-d'œuvre* of their kind, and while many passages exhibit naive traits, there is a spirit and vigor in the composition, very fascinating. Mr. LaRue has done full justice to Mr. de Gaspé in this paper.

Les fêtes patrônales des Canadiens-Français, is a pleasing history of the different fête-days observed in Canada including those of the patron saints. The origin of the name *Jean Baptiste*, so often applied to the French-Canadians, is given as follows: during the war of 1812, an English officer while calling off the rolls of the militia, noticed the frequent recurrence of the name *Jean Baptiste*, and turning to one of his comrades, said, "D—n them, they are all *Jean Baptistes*," which appellation has clung to them ever since. Mr. LaRue informs us that *Saint Joseph* was the first patron saint of Canada, and that he was afterwards supplanted by *Saint Jean Baptiste*, who was first known as Saint Jean, the first of whose fêtes took place at Quebec, on the 23rd June, 1646, as stated in *Les Relations des Jésuites*. The different ways of celebrating that day in several parishes are described by the professor, and are certainly interesting to us of the present age. Mr. LaRue attributes the motto, *Nos Institutions, Notre Langue et nos Lois*, to Mr. Etienne Parent, and refers to other details, equally absorbing which want of space alone prevents my noticing.

Les Richesses Naturelles du Canada, written in 1869, gives an excellent account of our great resources, with the expression of the opinion by the author, who, from his scientific attainments, in this particular department, should be an authority that Canada is one of the richest countries in the world. He tells us that we have gold and other metals in abundance. All we require to develop these resources and bring wealth to our doors are a market and capital, which, in the course of time, must inevitably be found. He assures us that we have within our territory everything requisite to secure prosperity, and prophecies a brilliant future for the Dominion. But he deprecates the course pursued by the *habitants*, in neglecting to enrich the soil, and says that they must be taught the evil of such neglect. He appeals to the Government to prevent the rapid destruction of our forests. The question of annexation is also treated, but no new light is thrown upon that subject.

L'Agriculture dans la Province de Québec, and *De l'Étude et de l'Enseignement agricoles*, published in 1869, are two papers deserving the closest attention, inasmuch as they refer to subjects on which depend the prosperity of our province, and are expounded by a gentleman who has made them his especial study. The development of the agricultural wealth of this country, must necessarily depend upon the knowledge brought to the task. Mr. LaRue says that " Canada is and ought to be an agricultural country, that the soil is of unequalled fertility, and that the most important grains and cereals necessary to man, here grow and arrive at full maturity in rich harvests." To the objection that our winters are too long, he replies, "it is well that it should be so; for, through stabling cattle, the farmer is enabled to procure manure for the enrichment of his land." This reasoning may appear farfetched to some. He emphatically affirms, that if there be poverty among the agriculturists, it is entirely due to their ignorance of the rotation of crops and the knowledge of farming. To people our country with farmers, who would get the best yield out of the soil and still maintain its richness, he suggests that the government should appoint a commission of competent men, one for each district, whose mission should be to investigate the systems in use and point out their defects and the means of removing them, in a report, which should be printed and distributed gratuitously to the farmers in the localities thus inspected. He also urges that the elements of agriculture be taught in all rural primary schools, and he gives other equally good and sound advice, which, if adopted, would doubtless bring about satisfactory results. The late Mr. François Perrault advocated this and practically carried it out in his schools as early as 1828.

L'Association de Médecine Canadienne. This paper treats of professional matters, but that portion of it referring to public hygiene and sanitary statistics must be interesting to all. The author's opinion, in 1867, on the sanitary condition of our public buildings, schools and hospitals, is not a flattering one by any means, but on the contrary rather alarming. He states that in none are the laws of ventilation observed, and the results are disastrous, as evidenced by the tedious convalescence of patients and the loss of health by pupils. The doctor loudly calls for legislation to remedy this crying evil. I fear that Mr. LaRue has had no cause to change his opinion since he wrote. As regards hospitals, however, he could certainly except the Jeffrey Hale, which, under the able management of Dr. Racey, has ever been a model one, not only in reference to ventilation, but in many other respects.

Whilst legislation is imperative on the subject of statistics, the doctor regrets that nothing has been done by the authorities to obtain complete returns of prevailing diseases, the influence of climate and seasons on the different races inhabiting the Dominion, the causes of disease and duration of life. The country should be in possession of such information and agitation kept up until it be obtained.

Some may be surprised to hear that the author believes that "no race is so little afflicted with pulmonary consumption, or longer-lived than the French-Canadians." To these facts and the proverbial prolificness of his countrymen, he ascribes their astonishing increase in numbers—from 60,000 at the time of the cession, to nearly a million in 1867, and this without the aid of immigration. Since Dr. LaRue's writing, these figures have been considerably increased; it is now stated that the French-Canadians number nearly two millions in Canada and the United States. The author, therefore, concludes that they are destined to play a most important *rôle* on this part of the American continent.

Coup d'oeil sur l'état actuel de la Médecine and *l'Iliade et la Médecine* are on a theme, which the confrères of the doctor will fully appreciate. They are written with that acumen and knowledge which might be expected from a man of his intellect and experience.

Scènes de Moeurs Canadiennes, are in three parts and form interesting studies of the life, customs and habits of the *habitants*.

First, *Les Danses rondes* is a graphic description of a Sunday evening, spent in a country house. The moment the guests are assembled, they discuss the merits of the sermon preached by the *curé* at *la grande messe*, and comment upon the marriages and deaths announced. Then follow the events of the day, which are fully canvassed. Next come games of cards, in which all join except the lovers, who prefer flirting in the corners; but the children are restless and must be amused, and the old people get up a round dance. When they are tired, the grand-parents assemble them and tell stories eagerly listened to by the wonder-struck and gaping little ones. Other amusements are provided, such as games of forfeit, blind-man's-buff, and similar innocent pastimes; finally, *la tire* is passed

round, when, shortly afterwards, the party breaks up—all
satisfied with their evening's pleasure. The behavior of
the children, the description of games and the toilettes are
given with accuracy and animation.

Second, *Chansons d'Enfants* is a brief notice of French-
Canadian nursery rhymes. To my mind they are inferior
to their English rivals. Nothing in them can equal " Sing
a song of Sixpence," " Old Mother Hubbard," and " There
was an old woman who lived in a shoe. These, apart
from amusing children, stimulate memory and develop
intelligence and should be in the hands of them all.

Third and last, *L'Isle d'Orléans*. Mr. LaRue pleasingly
dwells upon the attractions of this island. No one ought
to know it better than himself; he was born and passed
his boyhood there. He gives many important details
concerning its early traditions and history, which will prove
useful material to future writers on the island. With this
paper, the author closes this highly interesting volume.

Dr. LaRue is a lively and facetious writer; science and
art are happily blended in his compositions. Accurate
and felicitous exposition of ideas render his works, which
in parts would be dry and technical to the general reader,
as interesting as the "last new novel." His style is
original and at times laconic, and the old French idiom is
loyally observed; his diction is pure; nothing offensive
to the best literary taste being found in his descriptive
statements, or turns of thought. Possessed of a clear and

cultivated mind, he makes his meaning understood at once, by lucid and appropriate expressions. His *mélanges* have a value for style, wholly apart from their practical information, but, as a friend of mine observed the other day, "*le docteur, tout en étant un écrivain charmant, est toujours doublé du ' Médecin malgré lui,' de Molière.*"

PHILIPPE AUBERT DE GASPÉ.

It speaks well for the salubrity of our climate that a man of the ripe age of seventy-six could compose such a book as *Les Anciens Canadiens*, full of the recollections of the past and teeming with anecdotes and legends of that chivalrous period, when the settler had to be as skilful with the rifle as with the spade, and ready at any hour of the day or night to lay down his life in defence of his hearth and home. The author with a memory as fresh and active as when the events occurred narrates them with the force and energy which characterized his share in the incidents of the olden time. Not only his own lively adventures does he recount, but those of others as they were related to him, of some of the most important incidents of the last century, so rich in momentous transactions. Mr. de Gaspé weaves his reminiscences into a romance in which the reader is told that the son of a seignior, M. d'Haberville, and a Caledonian youth, Archie of Lochiel, form a friendship whilst pupils at the Quebec Jesuits' College, which, despite adverse circumstances, lasts through life. They spend their vacations at the Manor House at St. Thomas, of which an interesting description is given; the *salon*, the principal rooms and the out-buildings, creating the impression that such mansions must have resembled the feudal *châteaux* of the old world. Archie's character may be illustrated by a daring act, by which he rescued a man from drowning, on the occasion of the breaking up of the ice on *La Rivière du Sud*, at St. Thomas, while on a visit to his friend — Jules d'Haberville; a deed which gained for him the undying respect of the *censitaires* of the seigniory. The scene is graphically described with all its harrowing incidents: how one Dumais, while crossing the river in his carriole, breaks through the ice, and horse and vehicle disappear; but he himself succeeds in leaping upon a block of ice and escapes death; his leg, however, is caught in a *crevasse* and broken. One Captain Marcheterre, on his way home to the village that evening, ascertaining what had occurred, runs for help. Soon afterwards a tremendous crash follows and the ice suddenly moves and Dumais is helplessly whirled downwards with the glacial mass. Hundreds of pitying spectators on shore witness his perilous position; the alarm bell from the church steeple dismally peals forth its sad summons, and in despair the doomed man waives his adieux. The priest recites the prayers for the dying and grants him absolution. The scene becomes still more appalling; the rushing ice of the *Rivière du Sud* comes into violent collision with that of *Rivière du Bras*, a tributary of the former; for a few minutes the whole mass remains stationary, but, again it moves, and carries along with it the unfortunate Dumais. This tragedy is visible by the light of scores of flaming torches borne by the horrified spectators on the shore. The despairing man's wife arrives, melting all hearts by her frantic appeals to save the father of her children—but, in vain, courage fails all. The hummock, bearing Dumais strikes against the solitary tree of a submerged island in mid-stream, which he seizes in wild despair and swings in mid-air. At this crisis, Archie arrives and instantly takes in the situation and resolves to save Dumais, or " die in the attempt." He coils a rope around his body, jumps into the river, and, after daring and repeated efforts, which for a time seem fruitless, he saves the man whose strength was fast failing. The incidents of this thrilling episode are depicted with true and impressive skill. The customs and habits of the seigniors are charmingly sketched; their ceremonies, dignity and banquets receiving ample notice. The *fête* days at such manor-houses were observed with feudal splendor—*La fête de Mai* and that of *St. Jean Baptiste* were particularly honored; nor are the festivities of the kitchen nor the roysterings in the hall in those good old times forgotten.

Near the manor lives a M. d'Egmont, a gentleman who had spent his fortune in profuse and lavish entertainments to a horde of ungrateful and selfish so-called friends, who deserted when misfortune overtook him. One only remained faithful and mindful of previous benefits, an old valet, a foster-brother, who retires with his master to a cottage at St. Thomas and supports him from the savings laid past in his employment. From M. d'Egmont the author extracts much misanthropic philosophy, which, however, is assumed, as he is kind and gentle to all. On the estate also lives a sorceress, who foretells disaster to the youthful seignior and his sister, Blanche, and almost curses Archie, as one certain to bring misery to the d'Haberville family,—predictions which, strange to say, are afterwards painfully verified. Mr. de Gaspé sketches the whole history of the genus sorcerer at that time, and mentions many instances with that of Corriveau, who, after being hanged on the Plains of Abraham for murder, was exposed at Levis in an iron cage. He then proceeds with his tale ; matters run smoothly enough with the youths till they adopt the career of arms, one in the French and the other in the British army. In the course of events, Archie, a subaltern in the army of Wolfe, is obliged in the performance of his military duties, to destroy the villages and houses on the south shore of the St. Lawrence ; the manor house of the d'Haberville family, in which he had received so many kindnesses, shares the same fate as that of others. Whilst Archie is sadly contemplating the ruin and devastation, of which he had been the involuntary perpetrator, and upbraiding himself for his part in that wanton and cruel act, he is captured by Indians, among whom he afterwards recognizes Dumais, whose life he had saved, and who repays the debt by obtaining his liberty. On the heights of Ste. Foyo, April, 1760, Archie and Jules meet, the latter now a bitter enemy, under the conviction that his friend had proved a traitor. Meantime M. d'Haberville is obliged to accept the hospitality of the recluse, M. d'Egmont, for the war has ruined him ; but through the influence of Archie, he regains his property. After mutual explanations, friendly relations are restored between Archie and his old friends, and Archie proposes to Blanche, but her patriotism forbids the acceptance of an *Anglais* as a husband ; to which determination she adheres, despite her brother's pleadings. Archie resignedly accepts his fate and purchases a property in the vicinity of the d'Haberville seigniory, and settles into a a staid Canadian farmer, with Dumais as chief assistant. Archie and Blanche for many years pass their evenings in such social amusements as playing chequers. So ends this charming book. The author gives, in an appendix, many important and valuable notes.

The life and movement peculiar to Mr. de Gaspé's anecdotes and descriptions prove his actual connection with them, or his inspiration by the real actors. *Les Anciens Canadiens* forms but a part of a still more fascinating work of the author, his *Mémoires*, in which we have further information as to the generous hospitality dispensed in those days, and other details of the inner life of the old Canadians, pregnant with animation and local color.

It is unfortunate he did not earlier cultivate literature, his present achievements showing what treasures might have issued from his wonderful memory, vigorous intellect and felicitous pen. Mr. de Gaspé does not excel in mere style, but his more solid qualities, as well as his *verve* and *entrain*, compensate for any disappointment on this score.

ABBÉ E. D. BOIS.

This reverend gentleman possesses literary and antiquarian tastes, effectively noticeable in the writings which have flowed from his pen. He is animated by the literary spirit which manifests itself mainly in the interest of history and learning. Not desirous of public notoriety, his good taste is equalled by his modesty which shrinks from the publication of his name in connection with his works. Even the book about to be reviewed does not bear his signature. He is a careful and reliable recorder of events, his facts and dates being set forth with clearness and in a way to prove helpful to the annalist and historian.

Under the title of *Le Colonel Dambourgès*, the author writes the biography of one whose military and patriotic services were not, he believes, appreciated at their full value. François Dambourgès was born in 1742 at Salies, a small town in the department of the *Basses-Pyrenées*, where he was educated; but, being active and adventurous and brought into contact with the Basque fishermen, who were wont to follow their calling on the banks of Newfoundland and elsewhere, on the American coast, he became fired with the ambition of trying his fortune in Canada, where he arrived in 1763, and opened a sort of general store at St. Thomas, Montmagny. He so prospered that, in 1767, he returned to France and brought out with him his father and brother. In the war between England and her rebellious colonies, the services of M. Dambourgès were accepted by the government and he was detailed to harass the American hordes sent to invade Canada. He shortly afterwards received a captaincy in the *Royal Emigrants*, under Colonel McLean.

On the 31st December, 1775, Montgomery and Arnold attempted to carry Quebec by assault. The former met his death at *Près de ville*, and, in the attack upon the barricades at *Sault au Matelot* street, the latter was wounded. The city was defended by but sailors and marines belonging to the vessels in port, the Royal Emigrants and the Canadian militia, altogether amounting to about fifteen hundred men.* Although Arnold was *hors de combat*, his men endeavored to force the barricades, and took possession of the houses beneath the cliff, from which they poured their volleys into the defenders' ranks. It was at this moment that M. Dambourges distinguished himself. Procuring a ladder, and accompanied by but a single follower, named Charland, he effected an entrance into a house through an attic window, and cleverly captured thirty prisoners. His example was followed by Major Nairn in another building. Thus through the bravery of these two men the contest was brought to a close. The prisoners

---

* The official statement of the total number of men bearing arms gives eighteen hundred.—THE AUTHOR.

taken numbered four hundred and twenty-six, and there was also a large number killed. The besieged lost but five and two wounded. For this act of heroism M. Dambourgès received a commission in the 84th Regiment, which was, however, some short time afterwards, disbanded. He was subsequently elected a member of the legislature, but refused re-election, in order to accept an appointment in the Canadian Volunteers. After this he received a commission in the Grenadiers of the regular army. In the course of his military duties he contracted an illness from which he died in the city of Montreal, on the 13th December, 1798.

In this book, are published letters from James Thompson, Colonel L. DeSalaberry and J. Hale, which testify to the gallant behavior and bravery of M. Dambourgès, at the time of the seige. His widow received a pension of £30 sterling, during her life, from the British Government, in recognition of his distinguished services.

When the Prince of Wales visited this country, a petition was presented to him on behalf of the Dambourgès family, who were in great distress, but when His Royal Highness made enquiries as to the nature of the services of M. Dambourgès, he could receive no satisfactory information. To supply this want the present book was written.

The historical details are to the point and ample enough for the purposes of the writer. The diction is pleasing and the style simple. It will repay perusal, as interest and history are agreeably combined.

M. FAUCHER DE SAINT MAURICE.

One of the most original writers of the day in Canada is Mr. Faucher de Saint Maurice. He especially excels in recounting incidents of travel, of which he gives his readers a faithful record, displaying powers of observation and an amount of knowledge, industry and literary ability of a marked character. In a variety of respects, his writings are striking, of which I will give abundant evidence in this *résumé* of his abbreviated works. In France, there is hardly a French-Canadian writer better known and more generally appreciated ; in support of which I may mention the distinction conferred upon him, a few years ago, by his appointment to an honorary membership of *La Société des Gens de lettres de France*, accorded only to distinguished writers.

A la veillée, contes et récits, by the above-named gentleman, is a collection of short sketches, in which he gives free rein to his imagination. There is a delicacy of sentiment and refined humor, very characteristic of the author, which any one privileged to intimately know him will readily recognize as peculiarly his own. The first is entitled *Né pour faire un Monsieur*, and graphically depicts an evening in a *habitant* house of a Lower St. Lawrence parish.

There are here recorded personal experiences of imaginary feats, eclipsing even those of Baron Munchausen. Marvellous exploits in shooting and fishing—subjects always rather trying to the virtue of veracity—are narrated with the *sang-froid* and *vraisemblance* of a Gascon, and listened to without an incredulous smile on the part of the hearers. These yarns are occasionally varied by an old-time song or ballad, and at intervals moistened by a *larme de rhum*. Mr. Faucher is an adept in this species of composition, more apparent, perhaps, in his conversation than in his writings, giving faithful pictures of the long winter evenings in the old rural settlements of Quebec, their games, jests and pastimes, which are usually followed by fervent family prayer.

L'Amiral du Brouillard is an imaginative account of the loss of Sir Hovenden Walker's fleet, and forms a striking contrast to the admirably written historical version of that disastrous expedition, which will be hereafter reviewed.

Le feu des Roussi is a well-rendered tradition of the *Baie de Chaleurs*, concerning the courtship and marriage of a reformed rake to a true and virtuous girl, who dies from the effects of an accidental scalding, previously receiving from her husband a promise never to indulge in spirituous liquors. In this good resolve he leads a steady life, but unfortunately a friend of his wild youth visits and accompanies him on a fishing excursion. When far from land, a storm overtakes and drenches them with a freezing rain. Almost paralyzed with cold, the fisherman is tempted by his friend to take some rum to revive warmth. The next morning, the boat is found bottom upwards; and to this day a phantom light haunts the spot where Roussi broke the pledge he gave his dying wife. The story is well told by Mr. Faucher, but it is not stated, how it came to be known that Roussi had actually broken his promise, inasmuch as neither of the dead returned to tell the tale. Since penning the above, I have had occasion to refer to the author's work, *A la Brûnante*, which contains the tale of *Roussi* in its entirety. In the latter, the writer concludes his story more consistently: the tempter is saved, and it is he who relates it.

Le fantôme de la Roche is also a tradition of an after-death appearance of a debtor, who in his lifetime had promised a Fraser to acquit his debt, whether dead or alive. He had gone on a hunting expedition, when death overtook him; and the creditor was terrified one evening to see the ghost of the departed, who notified him of the fact of his decease, and how to obtain payment of the debt due him. It is said by the peasantry that no Fraser dies without the reappearance of this spirit.

Mon ami Jean is a tale of youthful friendship, and separation. One party enters matrimony and becomes "the head of a family;" but poverty begins to harass him, and he seeks relief in exile. In rapid succession follow distress, destitution, illness, loss of children, the death of his wife in an hospital, the disposal of her body to the dissectors, his own decease in the same institution and a pauper's grave. A sad, sad picture, but too common in this "vale of tears;" the gloomy effect of which is enhanced by the graphic skill of the author, who sweeps the chords of human suffering in the deepest diapason.

Dodo l'enfant depicts a family meeting around the evening hearth, when the traveled son describes an audience granted him by his Holiness, the Pope, and the emotions it aroused. The gentle words, which the head of the Church addressed to him, and the thoughtful enquiries concerning what he called "*mon pays de prédilection*," indelibly impressed upon his mind, are repeated to the circle, and listened to with fervent admiration. The *chapelet béni* is produced and assurances reiterated that it is the very same given to him by the Holy Father. The death of the old *grand'mère*, the void she leaves behind her and the scene on the occasion of the burial are rendered with a delicacy of feeling infinitely touching. The question asked by the little grandson beside the grave, "Why is *grand'mère* lying there and men throwing earth and stones upon her?" will bring tears to many eyes.

Le Crucifix outragé, is an account of a trial in Montreal in 1742, for sorcery and sacrilege, when the accused, Flavart, was convicted and condemned to kneel at the principal door of the parish church, in his shirt, bareheaded, with a cord round his neck, holding a lighted wax taper in his hand, and to declare in a loud voice that he had wickedly and sinfully profaned the words of Our Lord Jesus Christ; also to be beaten with rods, to be sent to the galleys for three years, and to be banished from the district for a similar period. The crucifix, which was desecrated in this manner, is now in the possession of the sisters of the Hôtel-Dieu, in this city.

Mexico. This paper is an enquiry into the origin of the ancient Mexicans, and in a brief space exhibits much research. The inferences, however, are merely hypothetical, as there are no means of arriving at safe conclusions on the subject;—mere legends being unreliable material. In their religion are traditions of Adam and Eve and of the flood; and in it is acknowledged the existence of the one God, who rules all things and is omniscient. The doctrines of baptism, symbolized by the sprinkling of water, which purifies and regenerates, and of the Cross, are professed; but with them are associated the horrors of human sacrifices and anthropophagism. The author gives a vivid description of the *fête*, *L'Ame du Monde*, in which, out of a host of prisoners, is chosen one, who to them is perfect in form and beauty. For a year, he is supplied with every luxury and all his tastes gratified; he is laden with gifts and honors and even worshipped and adored. Costly raiment is provided him and a continual feast is his;

while six of the most beautiful virgins of the country are given him as wives. The rich fawn upon and the poor bow down before him; he is more than a king, he approaches a god. But the end comes and on the fatal day, when the year expires, he is taken in a boat, attended by six priests, one of whom is clothed in a blood-red robe, to a temple on the border of a deserted lake, where he is stripped of all his grandeur and seized on by five of the priests, while he of the red garment cuts open his breast and takes from it his palpitating heart and offers it up to the god. In the evening, his remains afford a feast to princes, lords, and high dignitaries. In this nation, flourished the sciences, arts, painting, and poetry! Of the creoles the author does not seem to be enamored, unlike many other writers, who describe them as of perfect beauty and excellent taste. The men of this nation have a mixture of Spanish pride and Indian cupidity, while their passions are vices of the worst kind. When not embroiled in revolutions, they endeavor to acquire wealth by illegal means, in order to gratify their inordinate love of gambling, which is the ruin of all classes. Mr. Faucher mentions the case of a once wealthy man, who is to-day a beggar in the streets. In one night's sitting, he lost land, money, the carriage and horses waiting for him at the door, his servants' liveries and his own wardrobe. They are mean, vindictive, rancorous and fanatical, without energy, or honesty. Bull-fighting and the cock-pit are their principal amusements; their farms are neglected to carry on the better paying calling of highway-men. From 1538 to 1864 Mexico has had sixty viceroys, two emperors, three dictators, and thirty-one presidents, and political changes have been incessant.

This book mentions other attractive events and incidents, which limited space forbids my treating, and is written with a freshness aud vigor, which add to the pleasure derived from its perusal.

Deux ans au Mexique, published in *La Revue Canadienne* in 1864, and subsequently in 1874, in book form, is the diary of a stirring period, during which Mr. Faucher played a part, however modest, in the world's military and civil affairs, in this much distracted country. In the former and present edition the author continues the history of the events, which transpired after his departure from Mexico, such as the death of the ill-fated Maximilian, the trial and condemnation of General Bazaine, etc., thus making his work a complete record to the very time of publication. The period, to which it refers, is that connected with the struggle between Maximilian and Juarez for the establishment of the rival systems of imperialism and republicanism; Napoleon's powerful aid being given to his Austrian *protégé*. The American war ended, the influence of that republic was thrown into the scale of the native, or Mexican party, whose war-cry was liberty and self-govern. ient, with the result of overthrowing the imperialists, who claimed to be the party of order and true liberty, and bringing the unfortunate Maximilian to a traitor's death. The restoration of the *régime* of cutthroats and robbers, Mr. Faucher states to have been the outcome of the contest. The preface of this abbreviated edition, now under review, is by M. Coquille, the editor of *Le Monde* of Paris, in the finished style of that well-known writer. A participant in the struggle, the author enjoyed the best opportunities of judging of the merits of the quarrel, as well as those of the combatants and of witnessing and describing the extraordinary condition of the country during his residence therein. He was attached to the staff of General D'Hurbal, with the rank of captain, in the 2nd batallion, Light Infantry of Africa, and in constant communication with the officers and soldiers of Maximilian's army. In relating his experiences, he gracefully conducts the reader behind the scenes, introduces him to the leading characters *en deshabillé*, as it were, and exposes the springs of important events.

In 1864, Mr. Faucher reaches the city of Vera Cruz, which he finds squalid and repulsive, a very different picture from that presented from the steamer's deck on entering the harbor, when "distance lent enchantment to the view." Armed with his despatches he leaves for Mexico, arriving at the village of Soledad by train, and thence travelling by diligence. At the village of Camerone, on the route, sixty-two men of the foreign legion had distinguished themselves by sustaining a siege in a *hacienda* against two thousand four hundred Mexicans; lieutenant Maudet, with seven men, had at the point of the bayonet, compelled a large body of the enemy to retire, and covered his retreat into an outbuilding, where he and his companions heroically died. Ascending the Cordilleras, the author is thrown into ecstasies by the profusion of nature's beauties and wonders, the grand variety of the flora, the delicious fragrance of the woods and the wondrous diversity and brilliancy of the plumage of the feathered songsters, whose notes thrilled in choicest melody. At Orizava, he meets with a begging admiral and purchases cigars from a general of brigade— representatives of the vicissitudes of fortune. He finds the city of Mexico filled with a nondescript horde of all nationalities in search of personal advantage. The National Museum presented a valuable and strange, but ill-arranged collection ; from the half-buried cities of Mexico, Yucatan and Honduras, monolith monuments, temples, hieroglyphics found in the depths of the forest, eloquent of a long past and unknown civilization. If a Champollion (the discoverer of a key to the Egyptian hieroglyphics) could be found for Mexico to decipher the innumerable Aztec hieroglyphics already discovered and yet to be discovered, the advantages to archæology and science generally would be very great, and I hope that such a one may yet appear from amongst that phalanx of scholars who are daily startling the world with revelations from the forgotten and hitherto unknown. Affinities have been noticed between the languages of these countries and those of the Algonquins, Chinese and Finns. The monastries and convents contained valu˞ble MSS. and paintings, which were daily being destroyed by the bandit iconoclasts of that land of anarchy and misrule. The author here eulogizes Maximilian for his devotion to science, archæolc gy, poetry and art and for his chivalry and courteous urbanity. He was a bibliophile; he had collected seven thousand volumes, all bearing upon America, which by a faithful friend were transported when danger was imminent, from the palace in Mexico to Europe, where the collection was afterwards sold in the city of Leipsic.

In the town of Tacubaya the author becomes intimate with Prince Augustin de Iturbide, the youngest son of the first Emperor of Mexico (who was shot by his own people), a colonel of cavalry in the Mexican Lancers. When a child the prince had visited Quebec, and was pleased to frequently recall the occasion. His erudition and wit made him a charming companion and a great favorite. His untimely death, which occurred later, calls from the author an expression of deep regret. In the park of Chapultepec are cypress trees five thousand years old— patriarchs, indeed. Near the town of Puebla once stood a penitentiary, which was destroyed by fire by order of General Ortega, on which occasion all the prisoners perished in their cells. A custom obtains in the latter city of decorating with flowers the street, in which a death has occurred, and in some parts of Mexico, when a child dies the *salon* is embellished with the most fragrant and the brightest colored flowers, and the greatest gaiety is indulged in, for "an angel has gone to heaven." Near Puebla is the holy city of Cholula, in which is a pyramid, *téocali*, whose base is twice that of Cheops. Here the author is offered for sale an extraordinary animal plant, with a miniature tree, leaves and flowers growing out of its back, of the same species as the *Cicada plebeia* of Linnæus. Mr. Faucher here treats his readers to a long and scientific dissertation on the subject. He next gives an account of the warlike operations of the campaign and siege of Oajaca, which commenced with a brilliant defence of the convent of San Antonio, under captain Noyers, who was surprised by the enemy while all but twelve of his men were bathing. The latter, when communicated with, although almost in a state of nudity, brilliantly charged their foes with the bayonet ten times successively; reinforcements happily arriving, the Mexicans were defeated with great loss. The troops of Juarez were a villainous crowd, pillaging churches and convents and ransacking private houses. On the 13th of January, Marshal Bazaine assumed command of the army. The siege of Oajaca continues, and surprises, ambuscades, and skirmishes follow each other rapidly, and the instances of personal bravery are frequent and graphically recalled by the author. In fact it is more to this branch that he confines himself, as also to descriptions of the country and its history, than to the strategic movements of the armies. Political events and the important changes, which took place during those days, do not seem to have interested him. The beauty of the country and its extraordinary fertility in all kinds of products are continual causes of wonder,—subjects entered into with *gusto*. At this siege, the author was wounded in the foot by a piece of a shell, from which, however, he rapidly recovered, and was on duty within a few weeks. He records the countless charities and kindnesses of the ill-fated Maximilian and of " poor Charlotte," who sent immense sums to be distributed to those who had suffered during the war. On the 9th of February Diaz surrendered Oajaca. When in possession of the city, the French were astonished at the stupendous preparations which had been made for its defence, and were unable to understand why the Mexican general had surrendered, when he might have successfully resisted an assault. Leaving three battalions to garrison the town, the French army returns to Mexico. Mr. Faucher, in relating the history of the siege, mentions the name of many friends, whom he made there, and sketches their career. These biographical souvenirs frequently end with obituary notices, and the recollections which he so faithfully reproduces and so touchingly portrays are of those who have gone to that "bourne whence no traveler returns." To a man of Mr. Faucher's fine sensibilities it must have been a cause of infinite sorrow that, in the many friendships, which he formed at that period of his life, death so often intervened and claimed its victims; and the melancholy vein, frequently met with in his writings, may be partly due to such oppressive influences and to shocks given by family affliction. Mr. Faucher has been reproached by certain critics as being too much inclined to sentimentalism in his writings; to all but his detractors the above will be a sufficient explanation.

The arrival of the army in Mexico is the signal for a succession of balls, parties, receptions, and *tertulias* (a species of at-home); which season of gaiety is, however, interrupted by orders for a march on Morelia, in the neighborhood of which several murders had been committed. The execution of the bandit chief Romero and four of his companions is an incident of those days; a man who at last met with a just retribution for his many atrocious murders and shameful depredations. A touching account is given of the death of three officers, who lost their lives in assisting at a fire. One of these unfortunate men was the Vicomte de la Brousse, an intimate friend of the author. This death renders Mexico unendurable to him, and he is delighted to receive orders to proceed to the interior, Saltillo, occupied by the Mexican general with a large force of infantry, cavalry, and artillery. Commanded to make a *reconnaissance* at night, in charge of sixty men, Mr. Faucher falls into an ambuscade; whilst wounded and insensible, he is taken prisoner. Upon recovering consciousness, he finds himself confined in the quarters of General Negrette. The next day, however, he is placed under parole for one year and exchanged, and shortly afterwards, the Mexican general abandons Saltillo to the imperial forces. His health, having suffered from his wounds and exposures, Mr. Faucher obtains leave of absence, and returns to Canada, where he says :—*"Je me suis aperçu que le bonheur sur terre gisait au sein de la famille."* Shortly afterwards he marries, and sends in his resignation, which is accepted, and thus closes his military career.

In *Deux ans au Mexique* the author evinces a thorough acquaintance with his subject. He is eloquent and lucid in his naratives, explanatory in his history and particular in his facts. He treats his subjects clearly, succinctly and vividly, and explains doubtful questions with perspicacity and discrimination. There is solid instruction submitted in the pleasantest form and with much naturalness.

Promenades dans le Golfe St. Laurent. In the height of a Canadian summer, with its broiling suns and oppressive nights, what more refreshing thought than a visit to the briny waves? The denizen of the hot dusty city yearns for a sight of what Disraeli calls "the melancholy ocean," but what more cheerful word-painters describe as the joyous, restless, bracing and inspiring sea? How pleasant to recall the delights of rowing, fishing, or cruising, with a steady hand at the helm and a cunning eye at the mainsail! No wonder the "salt water" is such a welcome subject to many, and a holiday in the Lower St. Lawrence, with its enjoyable opportunities of physical and mental recreation, ever cheerfully hailed.

This book is another *souvenir* of a trip made by the author and a few friends, on board of the Government steamer "Napoléon III." when distributing provisions and stores to the different lighthouses in the river and gulf of St. Lawrence, and is a revised edition of a volume published by the author in 1877, under the title of *De Tribord à Bâbord*. It is by far the most complete and attractive work, descriptive of the scenery and history of the gulf that I have seen.

I will endeavor to express something like a fair, if in color, somewhat appreciative opinion of its character and style. Here will be found much interesting information, well arranged, and in language both clear and concise, furnishing pictures of the life and incidents connected with the lighthouses and other important points in the gulf. Events, grave and gay, in the lives of the simple, contented, middle-aged inhabitants of these remote stations are sketched with effective skill, and in a way reproductive of picturesque elements and contrasts of light and shade. With the same artistic effect, are related anecdotes, traditions and historical facts full of illustration, illuminating solid information and dissipating dry and repellent ingredients. The chief attraction of such holiday sketch-books is a happy combination of fact and fancy, each element being treated so as to offset and heighten the charm of the other. Thus, on the one hand, the author presents useful information, and on the other, adorns it with flowers of imagination. The romantic stories and events of the olden time constitute a worthy addition to the historic literature of the country, sometimes flavored with pungent citations from old writers, or actors connected with these famed regions, whose deeds and utterances are thus made to contribute fresh pleaures to a generation, which could otherwise never have known them. So the old notabilities are rescued from oblivion, whose lively chronicles awaken curiosity in the dullest, and whose creative spirit repeoples with truthful and interesting characters, scenes that must else have remained unknown to us forever. Felicitous touches, happy instances and quotations thus vividly reproduce the eventful years of long ago.

This volume opens with a lively sketch of the author's *compagnons de voyage*, and the staff of the little steamship ; and at the outset the reader is satisfied that he has with him enjoyable company.

The figure-head i his work is *Agenor Gravel*, whose

bons mots and exuberance of animal spirits continually enliven the reader, and whose individuality is merged in the person of a very intimate friend of mine, whose *verve intarissable* and rare conversational powers I hope long to have the pleasure of enjoying.

As Mr. Faucher progresses on his voyage down the river, in the gulf, the island of Anticosti, and the archipelago of the Magdalen Islands, he notes down his impressions, describes the history of the localities with their traditions, the kind of life led by the fishermen and guardians of lighthouses, the shipwrecks along the coast, and a variety of other exciting details, in language choice and clear. The observant and well-informed tourist is evident in every page. The "Napoléon" soon reaches *Isle aux Œufs*, when the author's thoughts naturally revert to the dreadful shipwreck and loss of life in connection with Sir Hovenden Walker's fleet, the memorable year of 1711. This episode in our history is narrated by a master-hand, and will be read by historians with genuine delight. Melancholy reflections must inevitably recur to the reader when he recalls the many precious and promising lives which have been sacrificed on our shores to the god of war; of men, whose abilities, if utilized in other channels, might have exercised powerful influence over the human intellect. Mr. Faucher next describes the arduous labor and self-sacrifice of the keeper of its lighthouse, Léon Coté, and his family, who, when the machinery had become disarranged, took it in turn to revolve the light every minute and a half, during five weeks of the autumn of 1872, and five weeks of the following spring. The cold at times was so severe that their hands became numbed, but still the machinery had to be kept working to prevent the dangers, which might have followed to mariners, had the light not been visible. A very amusing interview between the author and Barthelemy Ier, is related in a happy manner. Each locality in the St. Lawrence has its reminiscences, and most of them are sad and gloomy. The author, at *Sept Isles*, is reminded of the sudden death of the late commander Têtu, so well and favorably known in Quebec, and which was a source of deep sorrow to him. The account is narrated with much pathos and forms a delicate tribute of friendship. Fox Bay has also its tale of horror: in 1818, thirty persons, the crew and passengers of the " Granicus," were cast away on that bleak and inhospitable shore. They all died of starvation, the last survivors having been obliged to feed on the dead. Their bodies were accidentally discovered by a trapper, who, finding a cord suspended from a rock and taking hold of it, was terrified by hearing the ringing of a ship's bell. Overcoming his fright, he followed the windings of the rope, and came upon the half-eaten corpses of the victims of this d'saster. In 1736, the French vessel " La Renommée " was stranded on the Island of Anticosti, with fifty-four souls on board, many of whom were lost when attempting to land. The survivors divided into two parties, one remaining on the island and the other proceeding to Mingan for assistance. It was winter, and the attempt to reach that difficult locality was nearly proving a failure, when, through the superhuman exertions made, under the greatest trials and deprivations, by the reverend Père Crespel, aid was finally obtained for the famishing and hopeless remnant. This is a most noteworthy passage, and is an excellent specimen of instructive condensation—a whole volume in about sixteen pages. At the lighthouse, on the west point of this Island, a touching scene occurs on the return of a son to his father, after a long absence;—a happy suggestion to a painter. A tragic incident, a child burnt to death in the woods, whither she had gone, unknown to her father, and which had been set fire to by him to clear his land, is pathetically narrated. Mr. Faucher gives a detailed history of the origin, operations and signal failure of the Forsyth company, of the Island of Anticosti, and he comments upon their wasteful extravagance in purchasing immense stores of unnecessary articles, which eventually had to be sold at a great sacrifice, bringing ruin to all concerned in that unfortunate enterprise. A biography of the great pioneer and discoverer, Jolliet, is also given and is deserving of attentive reading. Pieces of artillery of the seventeenth century found on the beach of the island, which the author believes to have belonged to one of the frigates of the ill-fated expedition of Sir William Phipps, would form objects of interest to antiquarians. Such mournful relics, strewn along the coasts of the gulf, tell their own tale. The name of the once dreaded Gamache, the *croquemitaine* of the island, naturally comes to the mind of the author, and he gives a short sketch of the life and mysterious death of this noted character. His wonderful career form pages that will figure in the future history of the place.

Isle aux Oiseaux was visited uy Jacques Cartier in 1534; at that time, as now, the resort of myriads of birds. The island is most difficult of approach, inaccessible except in the calmest of weather. From a boat, the adventurous traveler must take his chance of missing his footing in attempting to ascend an almost perpendicular ladder of ninety feet in height. On the summit of the rock is built the lighthouse. Mr. Faucher nearly lost his life there on one occasion whilst making this ascent; he suddenly became dizzy, and only by an extraordinary effort of his will he overcame the feeling. Provisions and stores are hoisted by means of an elevator. The vast number of birds' nests is a subject of increasing wonderment; they appear to the eye a collection of miniature towns. Useful information is given of the geology and resources of the Island of Bryon, as also observations regarding its people. Scientific men are of opinion that the archipelago of the Magdalen Islands originally formed but one, and facts are adduced in support of this theory. The Hon. Mr. Fortin's scheme of bringing these islands into telegraphic communication with the mainland is highly commended, and its utility demonstrated. The Island of Saint Paul is described; terrible ship-wrecks occurred there at various times. The government has built a lighthouse to obviate accidents in its dangerous neighborhood. On the 16th August, 1876, a water-spout, a stranger in the gulf, swept over the island, levelling buildings, wrecking vessels and damaging crops. This sudden phenomenal visitation is graphically described. Approaching Cape Breton, the author indulges his fancy by presenting before the mind's eye the royal city of Louisbourg, with its encircling walls of fifty acres in extent, which "rose to the sky like threatening giants;" there stood its cathedral, its theatre, its hospitals, its convents, its private residences, soldiery at their posts on the ramparts; there were heard the sounds of martial fife and drum amid the thundering roar of fire-belching cannon; its gallant ships of war, proudly sailing from its port undauntedly to meet the coming foe; the attack upon the city begins, and a conflict to the death ensues; but hope dies and the proud city capitulates. The stirring events of the past, the heroes and great men of that day are marshalled before him, and his imagination, further leading him on, he speculates upon what might have been, if Wolfe had not lived, if Montcalm had not died ! Mr. Faucher delights to recall these ancient times and their old associations, and he revels in the vivid portrayal of these scenes. The Acadians and their history conjure up a host of sympathetic memories, and their descendants, inhabiting the Magdalen Islands, find in the author a dauntless champion in their grievances. The land tenure laws weigh very heavily upon them, and are thought by Mr. Faucher to be even more severe than those of Ireland. He urges the Quebec Government to purchaso the islands from the Coffin family, to whose ancsetors they were donated by Lord Dorchester, in the name of the Crown. The author notices the similarity of the accent and dialect of these people to those of Gascony and of the banks of the Garonne. The same remark applies to the fishermen of Chezetcook, near Halifax, who, have not only preserved their old home accent, but their costumes unaltered from the time their forefathers left their native soil. It is not, therefore, surprising that Mr. Faucher feels a deep interest in these primitive people, who remind him of his happy sojourns in that old France, of whose glories in the past her children and their descendants, on both sides of the Atlantic, are so justly proud, and whose name to them is emblematic of all that is dear and honored. *Mille et autre choses*, of greater or less importance, figure in this volume. Moore's poem on Deadman's Island forms an appropriate peroration to a book, which may boast of the finish and sentiment of the poem on subjects, inherently in the domain of poetry and romance.

Les Provinces Maritimes—La Gaspésie is the continuation of *Les Promenades dans le Golfe Saint Laurent* of which it forms the second volume. The "Napoléon III" cruises onwards to Pictou for coal. Here the travelers are struck with the Presbyterian austerity with which Sunday is observed in this Scotch town. On the following day they visit Halifax, when the author explores the citadel, and is charmed with the magnificence of the view, which, he says, can not easily be forgotten. He visits the cemeteries, where he notices the singular custom of placing shells at the base of tombstones, which, he poetically interprets as a means of communication with the dead through their murmuring sounds. The market is characteristic; the vendors being of three distinct groups; the Indians, solemn and reserved; the negroes, demonstrative and childishly uproarious and decked in gaudy colors; and the whites, with each their peculiarities. The author, accidentally addressing an Acadian, is startled to find in him the descendant of a common ancestor, who had arrived in Quebec in 1669. A trip round the harbor enables Mr. Faucher to judge of its wonderful advantages, where all the fleets of the world could anchor in safety. On this trip he is sensitively reminded of an appalling disaster, which occurred in 1746, to a fleet sent to the relief of Acadia, of eleven vessels and three thousand men, which, in view of Chibuctou, now Halifax, was suddenly dispersed by a violent cyclone; some of them being driven as far as the Antilles and others wrecked on Sable Island. Again the fleet was about entering Halifax harbor, when a frightful epidemic broke out among the crews, eleven hundred of whom died, including the admiral, in forty days, making two thousand four hundred lost since the departure from Europe; and only four vessels of the fleet returned to France. Arriving in Truro, the heart of ancient Acadia, the author falls into a reverie, and the past unrolls itself before him. In 1604, M. de Mons witnesses the foundation of Port Royal, now Annapolis; Champlain next explores the *Baie Française* and the coast of Maine, and the colony is full of life and promise; but days of misfortune and trial are in store. Sir Samuel Argyll captures *Sainte-Croix* and destroys *Port Royal*; then follow quarrels, dissensions and combats, similar to those between the barons of the middle ages, and the many acts of oppression and their retaliation, familiar to historians, during which the Acadians are gradually weakened. After the capitulation of *Beauséjour*, they realize their inability to contend further with their enemies, and lay down their arms and devote themselves to agricultural pursuits. But their dispersion is decreed, on the 5th of September, 1755, it is harshly carried out by the English: families are divided, husbands torn from their wives, parents from their children and transported to all parts of the British colonies. This act of heart-rending cruelty is a blot upon the fair fame of England and forms the groundwork of Longfellow's beautiful poem, "Evangeline." Far be from me any desire to excuse England for this atrocious deed, but it will be remembered that the Acadians were a source of continual annoyance ever in open revolt and planning expeditions to destroy English power throughout the country; and besides, it would appear from history, that Great Britain was not the first to conceive such a method of reprisal, for Denonville, through his agent Callières, submitted to Louis XIV. a similar plan to be carried out against the New Englanders. In speaking of the mines, Mr. Faucher states that coal, iron, copper, gold, gypsum and silver were discovered long ago by the *coureurs des bois*. Thirty mines are now in operation representing a capital of twelve million dollars. The "Napoléon III" next leaves for Charlottetown, Prince Edward Island, which impresses the visitor with its broad, tree-shaded streets. He points out all the advantages that would accrue to the Dominion from the construction of the Baie Verte Canal. It appears that it is the intention of the Government to assume, at an early day, this undertaking and to adopt a very ingenious system of dockage, devised and submitted to them by a young and promising engineer, Mr. Eugene Bender of Montmagny, by which a great saving upon the original estimate will be realized. The steamer then visits the lighthouses at Capes Tourmentin, Cassie, near Shediac, Richibuctou and Escumin.

The second part treats of New Brunswick and the Baie des Chaleurs. Miramichi is difficult of access, but the Federal Government has greatly improved the entrance thereto. In passing, are seen on the port side Chatham, and on the starboard Douglastown, while in the distance is Newcastle, at which Mr. Faucher and party are cordially received. *La Tracadie* is next visited, where are, as it were, entombed, the victims of leprosy. It is described as having been a hell of blasphemy and obscenity, till six ladies, from the Hôtel-Dieu of Montreal, courageously determined to sacrifice themselves to the care of the patients afflicted with this dreadful and loathsome disease. It is stated that segregation is causing a great decline in the number of these outcasts. Relieving the lighthouse at Shippegan, the " Napoléon III" proceeds to the Island of Miscou, once, according to tradition, the haunt of a huge monster, in the shape of a woman, who was wont to devour the Indians wholesale, and by whom she was called "Gougou." The island now contains only about a dozen families. They next stop at Caraquette, the oysters of which are extolled, when they proceed to the Baie des Chaleurs and land at Dalhousie, the beauty of whose surroundings excites enthusiasm. A little beyond Dalhousie are points *A la garde* and *A la batterie*, near which, in 1760, a French fleet was destroyed by the English, who subsequently set fire to *Petite Rochelle.* Mr. Faucher relates the zeal of Père Le Jeune, among the Micmac Indians of the Restigouche, and quotes from Prof. Dawson of McGill University to prove the similarity of many words of their language to Greek and Latin. The author then relates the great service, rendered by the Rev. Edouard Faucher de Saint Maurice, an uncle of the author, to the English settlers of the Restigouche, when on that mission, by preventing their wholesale massacre by the Micmacs, through his influence over them and promises of redress of their grievances by the English government.

The third part of the work treats of *La Gaspésie.* Leaving Dalhousie they arrive at Carleton, where the lobster trade is carried on, on an extensive scale. He deplores the non-existence of a legal check upon lobster-fishing at certain seasons; for this fishery must eventually be destroyed by the present indiscriminate slaughter. In a geological collection of Mr. Meagher, he saw specimens of jasper, agates, red feldspar, syenite, porphyry and white, yellow and green quartz, found in the locality. At Paspebiac are the monster fishing establishments of the MM. Robin & LeBouthillier. At Port Daniel he falls into ecstasies over the beauty of the scenery, and being off Cape d'Espoir, he relates the loss of a vessel there, which he believes to be the " Feversham," of Sir Hovenden Walker's fleet. While at Percé Rock, he recalls its past and marvels at its millions of birds. He also alludes, in connection with the history of Percé, to two English frigates, which, in 1690, arrived there, when their crews landed and burnt the village and desecrated the church, using the altar and the sacred vestments in a sacreligious manner. At Pointe St. Pierre, is met the government yacht, *La Canadienne*, when civilities are exchanged. Gaspé Basin is next visited, characterized by Admiral Bayfield, as "safe as a dock." In 1628, Admiral Roquemont was defeated in its waters by Kirke. In 1711, Sir Hovenden Walker took shelter from a fearful storm, and in 1759, some of Wolfe's vessels revictualled here. The "Napoléon III" arrives on a gala day, for the Federal steamer "Druid," with His Excellency Lord Dufferin on board, whom the people enthusiastically welcomed. Mr. Faucher highly eulogizes this most popular governor, describing him personally and his eminent services to literature and his country. He refers to the petroleum mines of Gaspé and gives a description of Cape Rosier, relating the shipwreck there of the "Carrick," in 1847, when one hundred and seventeen immigrants were lost. The author lands at the Cape de la Madelaine, and refers to the famous *Braillard* and relates the legend how it was caused to cease by a reverend Father there resident, but who would never divulge the means he had adopted, nor his experiences on the occasion. Leaving the Cape, the "Napoléon III" steers for Quebec, to the delight of the travelers, notwithstanding their agreeable journey.

Mr. Faucher de Saint Maurice has been searching in his enquiries and his statements bear the stamp of truth. In his pleasant narratives and sketches, he has made use of facts and traditions with the best results, his humor not seldom illuminating both. This author has the faculty of happily expressing what his subjects felt and thought. His imagination revels in such descriptions as that of Isle de la Madelaine, Baie des Sept Isles and other scenes, whose attractions are enhanced " by thoughts that flash and words that burn." This book presents an elaborate mosaic, every fragment of which has been collected from the records of early settlers, original documents, manuscripts and letters, or to use another figure, Mr. Faucher's fine taste and unwearied industry have collected a mass of varied and fascinating materials, which, passed through the alembic of his mind, have issued in forms of practical utility and literary beauty.

I must congratulate the author upon the honorable recognition of the value of this book by the French Minister of Marine, who has ordered several hundred copies to distribute annually for ten consecutive years to the different libraries of the Department of Marine and naval schools.

I repeat, M. Faucher's style of narrative is felicitous, clear and graceful, flowing on like a smooth living stream. His contributions on Canadian history are valuable additions, throwing new light on passages hitherto somewhat obscure, and correcting errors touching the names of famous localities. While supplying fresh information on a variety of topics, and lucidly and briefly giving facts, difficult of access to the mass, thus exhibiting a practical spirit, his productions sparkle with humor and natural vivacity, in a way calculated to carry along the reader with exhilarating effect. His descriptive powers are excellent, as may be recognized when depicting landscapes, ocean scenes, coast adventures, and thrilling incidents of peace and war. Power of imagination and broad sympathies in unison with graphic skill are reflected in his works, giving them an intellectual flavor captivating to all. Where so much calls for the highest praise, it may seem captious to point out any blemish, if what I am about to mention may be considered such; but the reviewer has faithful duties to perform. The resort to reveries as a *mise en scène* is very effective, but its frequent repetition ought to be shunned. I would also suggest his avoidance in future of the employment of words not in daily use, for his diction renders his works somewhat difficult to those not very familiar with the French language. I hope our literature may receive many more contributions from the facile and brilliant pen of Mr. Faucher de Saint Maurice.

L. H. FRÉCHETTE.

Pièces choisies, is a small volume of selections from our national poet, who has lately received the highest honor in the gift of the Academy of Paris, for his poems, *Les Oiseaux de neige* and *Les Fleurs Boréales*. It is many years since he attempted his first poetic flight, under the title of *Mes Loisirs*, which won for him more than local fame. His writings are distinguished by a delicacy of thought, loftiness of conception, a felicity of expression and a purity of style, which evince the true soul of poetry, charming all its lovers.

In the stanzas *Découverte du Mississipi*, which is one of his finest efforts, the grandeur and the solemnity of the mighty river are powerfully impressed upon the reader:

"Le Roi-des-Eaux, n'avait encore....
. . . . .
Déposé le tribut de sa vague profonde,
Que devant le soleil et Dieu."

An eulogistic poem, addressed to the Abbé Tanguay, for heralding to the world names, otherwise forgotten, though meriting immortality, says :—

"C'est vous, savant abbé! c'est votre livre, ami
Qui se fait leur vengeur, et répare à demi
L'ingratitude de l'Histoire."

Two glowing poems, addressed to the favorite American poet, H. W. Longfellow and our Poet Laureate, Pamphile LeMay, are full of genuine admiration, forming a noble tribute of friendship to both.

Renouveau and *Le 1er Janvier* are poems of nature, replete with beautiful thoughts; as is also *Impromptu* written at Chicoutimi.

In the lines, *A ma soeur*, the poet lovingly dwells upon the beauties and charms of spring, and how welcome it will be to her in her youth, but how unmeaning and void to the exile, whose only balm is,—

> "Ce doux baume, trop rare, hélas !
> C'est l'assurance que là bas
> Quelqu'un nous aime ! "

Then follows *Sur sa tombe*, of the sister just addressed who has seen but ten of those glorious spring-times, and

> "C'était, dans son prisme vermeil,
> La goutte d'eau du ciel venue,
> Et qui remonte dans la nue,
> Avec un rayon de soleil ! "

La nuit and *Le matin* are two delightful pieces sparklingly brilliant. *A l'Eglise* is full of sympathy. *Alleluia* is a religious festival poem, which, some believe to be the most affecting of his effusions. It is addressed to M. L'Abbé Thomas Caron, V.G. *A mon filleul* and *A une enfant* are poems to youth and incline towards a melancholy view of life rather disheartening to the young; but hope is strong in its spring-time and even the poet's forebodings and discouraging advice can not crush it out:

> " Enfant ne sonde pas les secrets de la vie ;
> Helas ! reste toujours enfant !"

La dernière Iroquoise is a tragedy in verse, harrowing and awe-inspiring. A squaw not satisfied with the murder of a pale-faced child, but,

> " Comme un vautour féroce, aux entrailles s'attache,
> Lui découvre le coeur, de ses ongles l'arrache,
> Et le dévore tout sanglant !"

The recall of these horrors is revolting, although too frequent in the past of this country, but more æsthetic subjects are preferred in the present age.

Le lac de Beauport will revive many pleasant times and still dearer associations, never to be forgotten.

La forêt Canadienne is a subject on which Mr. Fréchette dwells *con amore*, especially in the glorious autumn. The beauties of the woods at that season " are a joy forever;" he revels in expressive words and brilliant metaphors. Some of these descriptions are perfect gems, poetically apostrophizing charming localities, so numerous in Canada.

There are several other choice pieces of the author not found in this volume. I miss especially *La voix d'un Exilé*, in which are many passages that would vie with the best of Victor Hugo's; but, unfortunately it contains allusions of such bitter enmity to political antagonists as to detract from their poetic effect.

Mr. Fréchette's verse is chaste and highly finished; pathetic or tragic, as he wills it. He excels, however, in descriptive *paysages*, events of olden times and love passages. In his *Mississipi*, he soars to the highest realms of fancy, displaying striking originality. Comparisons have frequently been made between him and our other national poet, the late Octave Crémazie. Fréchette, in his *Poésies choisies* is a rippling, woodland stream, and Crémazie, in his effusions, a roaring mountain torrent. One draws from his silver lute notes of infinite sweetness, and the other from his war trumpet calls to arms and ushers one into the heat of battle.

OSCAR DUNN.

Few who have followed the events of Canadian journalism need be reminded that one of the most accomplished contributors to our ephemeral literature is Mr. Dunn, whose compositions are usually marked by a spirit of liberality, as well as soundess of information, not frequent among writers of the press, in this country. Always desirous of retaining the pure idiom of the French language, he made an impression in Canada that was even reflected in Paris, on one of whose papers, *Le Journal de Paris*, under the control of the well-known M. Weiss, he occupied an influential position. In such a school and with his talents, Mr. Dunn could hardly fail of becoming a good writer. Whatever literary schemes this gentleman has in view, and I believe they are not few, nor discreditable to the reputation of *les belles-lettres* of Canada, he will always tell the truth for its own sake, and convey even unpleasant information in a language as polite and classical, as to excite the approbation of lovers of Massillon, Corneille and Racine. On the Paris press, Mr. Dunn's literary efforts were acknowledged as possessing merit, and it was a common remark, in that great centre of European art and taste, that that gentleman might have been born in Paris and educated in France.

Under the title *Lecture pour tous*, Mr. Dunn publishes a collection of papers and essays, dedicated to the memory of one of our promising *littérateurs*, the late Professor Lucien Turcotte, of whose short life he gives a brief sketch, complimentary alike to the head and heart of the writer.

The first paper in this series is on the question, *Pourquoi nous sommes Français*, written in 1870, at which time the French arms had suffered overwhelming reverses in the Franco-Prussian war. Mr. Dunn asserts that the French-Canadians, although politically English, are French at heart, a condition possible, he admits, through British liberty, which guarantees them their language, their religion, and their laws; England at the cession being glad to receive and proud to retain them on those terms. He next portrays the marked differences between the French and English temperament, the one being the antipodes of the other. The beauties of the French language are eloquently signalized, its preservation being, in a great measure, due to its gallant use in intercourse with *le beau sexe*, to the Roman Catholic clergy, in the work of Education, and to the legislature through its employment in official documents and debate, besides the action of the French-Canadian authors and journalists, with the same end in view. In remaining

French, he thinks, they become the agents of France and the Church, which has done so much for Canada, and thereby enjoy an influence in the world, which they would lose were they to divest themselves of their old nationality and become Anglicized, as Louisiana. This article has been frequently cited by prominent French writers, when treating of Canada, in a laudatory manner among others, MM. Rameau and de Bonnechose.

The second paper is also on the subject of nationality, entitled, *Nos gloires nationales,*. It recalls the glories of the past, and appeals to the French-Canadians in the United States to return to their native land, whose free institutions nearly approaches the ideal of enlightened lovers of liberty. He endeavors to impress upon them that it is their duty to remain in Canada, and be true to their traditions, their laws, their customs, and their religion. The effect of such eloquently stirring words must have been electrical, and with results in the direction aimed at.

The third paper is *Le pouvoir temporel.* Mr. Dunn is a true son of the Church, and a zealous and earnest supporter of the temporal power of his Holiness, the Pope. He argues that the Papal States, having been assigned by their princely rulers to the successor of St. Peter, not as a personal gift, but for the purposes of the Church, no vote of the Roman people could deprive him of them, and, that even were such admissible, every Catholic in the world had a voice in this matter as well as the small Roman minority, whose act was not a legitimate alienation. Mr. Dunn believes that Napoleon III., who was chiefly instrumental in depriving the Pope of his territory and power, met his deserts at Sedan ; Napoleon's countenance and aid brought about the unification of Italy, which led to the formation of the German Empire and its subsequent successful rivalry with France. By many it is looked upon as the fulfilment of the scriptural prophecy, that punishment will descend to the third and fourth generation, for it was Napoleon Bonaparte, who first conceived and carried out this policy, his nephew merely following out this policy. The picture of the venerable Pio Nono, " the prisoner of the Vatican," is touching.

The author's fourth paper is entitled, *L'Instruction Publique*, a subject which he is admittedly competent to handle, from his position as a chief officer of this department. He cleverly combats the theory that education in the colleges is too classical and not sufficiently suitable to practical life, but rather calculated to incline students to the professions. He contends that the best preliminary preparation for a commercial, or agricultural, career is a course of classics, which is the only sure basis for solid enlightenment. The mental training, secured by classical instruction, gives marked advantage to its possessor in the contest for the lead in all important movements. On the other hand, he acknowledges with regret, the general desire of farmers to push their sons into the professions, now and long overcrowded, under the mistaken and pernicious idea that there is something degrading in trade, or agriculture, which students after a college course are only too prone to believe. For the children of the poor, he advises the establishment of primary schools where agricultural chemistry, drawing, book-keeping, etc., would be taught. He praises the present system of education, but admits there are defects, which may be remedied by increasing the remuneration of school inspectors and teachers, and thus securing more competent men. He urges the immediate attention of the authorities to the subject, and recommends the establishment of mercantile schools in the cities of the province. Although some may differ from the author on a few points, his ideas are broad and liberal, and discussed in a fair spirit.

The last paper, *L'Amérique avant Christophe Colombe*, is an enquiry into the different traditions and accounts of the discovery of the people of America before the landing of Columbus. The traditions of the Egyptians and other ancient races, regarding the Island of Atlanta are dealt with in a pleasing style; the visits of the Basque fishermen receiving due notice.

The magnificent ruins of Central America and Guatemala, and the supposed derivation of their languages from the Sanscrit, or Aryan sources, and the similarity of their religions to those of Egypt, Greece and Asia Minor, are topics treated with erudition and skill. He thinks the American continent could easily have been reached from Asia by the Aleutian Islands, Behring Straits and Alaska ; and from the Atlantic by way of Scotland, the Faroe Islands, Iceland and Greenland. Archæological researches have proved that the Northmen visited America five centuries before Columbus, and found it inhabited by red men, propably of Asiatic origin. The names of several pirates and adventurers, who had visited various parts of America are given, who were there as far back as 725 A.D.; and there is mentioned the birth of a Northman in America in 1000, A.D.—483 years before Columbus. A description is given of the Dighton Writing Rock, found on the banks of the Taunton River, county of Bristol, Mass., U.S., with which is connected a very old tradition. As for Greenland, it was thickly settled in the tenth century, and in 1121 the first bishop was consecrated there. But a legend, in China, far outshadows all these. It refers to a country called Fou-Sang, evidently the west of America, being visited by the Chinese, 700 years before Columbus. Be they who they may, those who first discovered this continent found there before them inhabitants, whose history is unknown and whose origin is hidden in mystery. Mr. Dunn goes over the several theories in reference to this vexed question, but they are mere theories, and lead to no positive conclusion. To people of antiquarian tastes, in particular, much matter, both alluring and instructive will be found in this treatise.

Dix ans de journalisme is also by Mr. Dunn, and is a collection of able articles, culled from his many contributions, whilst a journalist. It is an acknowledged fact that, in proportion to the labor and research, necessitated in the preparation of an article, the author values his work ; and these papers, being the result of careful study and mature reflection, the author has rescued them from the oblivion, to which all effusions in the daily press are doomed.

The first in this volume discusses *L'Affaire Guibord*, which excited so much interest in Montreal some years ago. After a recital of the facts of the case, the writer proceeds to give his views, which are strongly in support of the position taken by the ecclesiastical authorities, who refused Guibord burial in consecrated ground, he having died while under the censure of the Roman Catholic Church. The cause of that censure was his connection with *L'Institut Canadien*, which has long been under the ban of the church. This society contended that no excommunication could deprive a citizen of the civil right of burial, and his widow appealed to the courts to compel the *curé* of the parish to give her husband sepulture in consecrated ground. The author discusses the whole question at length, including the right of the court to interfere and coerce the ecclesiastical authorities. He argues that canonical censure properly deprives the accused of any such rights. It is well to state here that the Institute was condemned on account of its possessing books on the *Index*; and an appeal to Rome on the subject resulted in the confirmation of the censure and a sentence of excommunication against all who continued members of the Institute. Mr. Dunn, therefore, concludes that its members, being fully aware of the judgment passed upon them, could not complain of their deprival of ecclesiastical rights, or privileges, if they remained disobedient to the church. He also contends that the civil law can not override the decrees of the church, especially as to the right of burial; that the union between church and state in Canada exists theoretically, as fully as under French rule; which means the supremacy of canonical decrees; that the civil courts can not pronounce in matters ecclesiastical; and that the excommunication of the church deprived Guibord of certain civil rights, by virtue of his loss of those ecclesiastical.

Notwithstanding the able arguments of Mr. Dunn, in behalf of the case of the church, the highest authority in the realm decided against it, and Guibord was buried in consecrated ground.

L'Union des Catholiques. In 1871, certain politicians

adopted what was known as the *Programme Catholique*, which many feared would affect the prestige of the clergy, weaken the influence of the Catholic community and create a split in the conservative party. This apprehension the author shared, and in consequence, he thought it his duty to give the warning in the treatise under review. The counsel contained in it may have had some influence, for subsequently the *Programmistes* disappeared from the political horizon. The author says that properly speaking, there is no nationality on this continent; we are simply composed of groups of different races which have not yet amalgamated. Immigration has thrown upon our shores "ready-made" citizens, with ideas already formed, with national prejudices, religious animosities and peculiar habits and customs. These widely different elements have lived amicably together, for each is bent upon amassing wealth. The contrast between the severe regimen of European customs and laws and the enjoyment of untrammelled libert have also co-operated towards this end. Immigration has prevented that assimilation to a homogeneous population, which would otherwise have been practicable. These various races, although living peaceably together and working unitedly for the public weal, still preserve all their home traditions and original traits. The author wishes that the Catholics would follow this example; but, he regrets to add, that they are far from united. Isolated and receiving no support from their co-religionists in the United States, their preservation demands their organization in a compact body. Politically speaking, to divide the Catholics is to divide the conservative party. Mr. Dunn points out that in our midst exists a dangerous school, Canadian rationalism, against which it is well to be warned. The French-Canadians, he says, have inherited from their ancestors, the Normans and Bretons, a love of litigation and a bickering disposition, and it is owing to this national characteristic that dissension exists in their ranks. Another cause is that Canadian Catholics, believing that they possess the sole truth, are inclined to be intolerant of adverse opinions among themselves, a dangerous fault aggravated, says the author, by political difficulties. One more evil is the confounding of Canadian with European politics, which often leads to misapprehension. The title conservative in one country may not mean a conservative in a wholly different one; there is more confusion however, in the use of the term liberal in France, Canada and other countries. A Canadian liberal, as regards his views on religious and moral questions, or ecclesiastical rights, might stand shoulder to shoulder with a French conservative. In France a liberal is a free thinker, rebelling against all religious authority; but, in Canada he may be an ultramontane. To avoid misconceptions with regard to foreign questions, parties, the author says, should be classified as conservatives, radicals and liberals; the latter appellation then would not be so distasteful to Catholics. Other causes of disunion include Gallicanism, real or imaginary. The clergy have never attempted to form a national church, since the civil code respects all its doctrines. Mr. Dunn foresees an anti-clerical reaction not far off, and to meet it he advises his co-religionists "*In necessariis unitas, in dubiis libertas, in omnibus charitas*, and above all things to avoid bitterness, for irritation is an evil counsellor."

Après le combat : union des partis politiques dans la Province de Québec. This paper was indited after the electoral contest of 1873, when the conservatives were defeated and the Mackenzie government came into power. Mr. Dunn thinks that in this struggle the liberals were aided by many conservatives, including not a few of their journals, and that the liberals formed but a fraction of the majority. To obtain their success the latter had departed from their usual tactics and encouraged the Catholic sentiment. The mass of the people, although supporting the liberal chiefs, was still conservative. He, therefore, concludes that the principles of liberalism were not triumphant; an anomaly, to be removed but by a fusion of parties. The author then discusses the possibility of such a fusion. He states that, as the national party coalesced with the liberals and favored confederation and independence, later, there is no essential difference between them and the conservatives. Confederation having created a new equilibrium of interest, race and religion, has considerably contracted the field of action, and consequently liberalism is not the same as before 1867; and the nationalists have not so far professed any radical principles, so that the conservatives can not object to a fusion with either of these parties; for neither conservatives nor Catholics have ever voted for divorce, or mixed schools, and there is no vital question at issue between them. Conservatives are in favor of confederation and as an indispensible adjunct, the construction of the Pacific Railway. The denomination of parties, at Ottawa, should be national conservatives and radicals. Mr. Dunn appeals to the Canadians to be united and thus avoid being subject to constant menacing control. The author claims that confederation was framed for this province alone, all the others at the time being in favor of legislative union. Through the energy and perseverance of Sir George Cartier, it was thus carried, ensuring to Quebec its peculiar institutions. He adds, that the construction of the Pacific Railroad is essential for the retention of British Columbia and Manitoba in the confederation; that they would otherwise secede and become annexed to the United States, which would break up the Dominion and end in annexation, which he would infinitely regret. Mr. Dunn also objects to Imperial Federation, as it would leave Canadians without a country, or, at any rate, with one that would not satisfy the aspirations of a people, predestined, sooner or later, to form an independent nation. He draws a picture of what Canada would be, if annexed to the neighboring republic, a mere state, without a nationality, and its people scattered in all directions, with their farms and houses in the hands of American speculators and a different language, religion and customs prevailing throughout the land. In this the author effectively appeals to his countrymen to rally and unite their forces for their national safety.

Then follow four papers on *L'Instruction Publique*. The first three have already been noticed in these reviews; the fourth is a *Pétition au Ministre de l'Instruction Publique*, in the form of a letter written, as it were, by an inhabitant of St. Xiste, who implores, in the name of humanity, assistance for a poor school teacher in that parish, who is eking out a miserable existence upon a mere pittance. The school-master is a young man of thirty, a graduate of the Normal School, the father of three children, possessing talents and enjoying the esteem and confidence of the respectable people of the locality, with a salary of three hundred dollars, to feed and clothe himself and family. He is almost starving. At one time, he nearly loses his situation; for one who could glibly read the *Devoir du Chrétien* offered his services as teacher for two hundred and fifty dollars. That year the parish had suffered losses, and economy was considered necessary and urged by the parishoners. This proposal was rejected by a majority of only one of the school commissioners. The teacher is so provoked at this indignity, that he threatens to leave, but is prevailed upon by friends to remain. He again conscientiously resumes his work of instructing the youth. On another occasion, he applies for an increase of salary, and is saved from dismissal but by the influence of the *curé*. Thus he continues struggling, and, being unfitted for any other work is without hope ; despondency takes possession of him and his pupils are neglected, for he has lost heart. "Will you not come to his aid, *Monsieur le Ministre?*" piteously cries the petitioner: "He will surely die of hunger, or be driven to desperation, if he be not aided by Providence, or the government." The great value of the services, rendered by that humble and unappreciated class in our community, is ably set forth, and an appeal made which should not be overlooked. The petitioner suggests that every primary school teacher, receiving a salary of three hundred dollars, or more, shall be paid an equal sum from the provincial Treasury. I agree with Mr. Dunn that it is indeed time that justice should be rendered so deserving a class. Retrenchment may be the order of the day, but it should not be practised at the expense of those, whose hardships are a crying evil in a civilized community like our own.

La Question Agricole. In this paper, Mr. Dunn taxes the French-Canadian farmers with extravagance in living, in neglecting the system of rotation of crops and manuring the land. He further deplores the absence of schools having proper agricultural instruction, and calls upon the *curés* to recommend to their parishioners prudence, frugality and moderation. He insists upon the instruction of the rising generation in agriculture, which will be simplified by the manual on that subject by Dr. LaRue, which has been widely distributed in the country parts. The author says, that the child should be taught a catechism of agriculture similtaneously with religion. In the province of Quebec this instruction is now obligatory from which the best results may be expected.

La loi électorale. In this paper, Mr. Dunn refers to the more salient points and objections in the working of this act. He assails the clause, requiring of members a property qualification of the value of two thousand dollars. In England it was considerably modified in 1838, and totally abolished in 1858. The solid qualifications of a member should be honesty and an interest in the country. The author is of opinion that senators and legislative councillors should be qualified by the possession of property, they being, in this country, where no aristocracy exists, the representatives of the landed interest ; a counterpoise and check to the elective chamber. In reference to the vote by ballot, Mr. Dunn says, that it will enable those, who receive money for their votes, to record them against the briber, and those, who are in fear, or in the power of another, to vote according to their conscience. In England, this method has been successful, while in the United States it has not failed, and in Nova Scotia, after a short trial, it has been abandoned for the old system of open voting. The author quotes approvingly the late M. Prévost Paradol's recommendation, that only those who write should enjoy the franchise, which would prove an incentive to education. This was advocated in 1840 by that educationalist reformer, the late Mr. Perrault. Mr. Dunn devotes a short space to compulsory education and its inevitable adoption in this country. The propriety of granting the franchise to educated people, to the members and students of the learned professions and to employés and others, who are in the receipt of four hundred dollars a year and over, is urged. The author believes the law against bribery and corruption is not too strict and predicts that it will be found efficient in securing purity of elections. On the subject of the oath, he gives several instances of its evasion, in reference to the receiving of bribes, such as presents to the elector's wife, or children, or purchase from him at extravagant rates. With respect to the word "indirectly," in the oath, he pretends, that it is not generally understood in its full meaning, and is often unhesitatingly taken by those, who have knowingly "indirectly" received bribes, but who are unaware that this is covered by the oath. Mr. Dunn's strictures on the act are well taken, but since his writing there have been many amendments, which have improved the operation of this law.

Charles Laberge. The subject of this short biography, Mr. Dunn says, was one of the distinguished band of liberals, who founded the *Institut Canadien*. Prominent in their ranks was this gentleman, who was born in Montreal, 20th October, 1827, and educated at St. Hyacinthe College; on leaving which, he was crowned by the Hon. L. J. Papineau, the then Speaker of the House of Assembly, for oratory. He was admitted to the bar in 1848. In 1852, he left Montreal and settled at St. Jean d'Iberville, where he soon formed a large *clientèle*. Mr. Dunn says, that he was the most brilliant contributor to *L'Avenir*, among many of the best writers in Canada. He was elected to the Legislative Assembly in 1854, as member for the county of Iberville, and took first rank in the group, of which M. Dorion was chief, who were known as *La pléiade rouge*. M. Laberge entered the Brown-Dorion administration as Solicitor-General, and, upon its fall, after an existence of but forty-eight hours, he retired from public life and devoted himself to the practice of the law. In 1863, he was appointed judge *ad hoc* to replace Mr. Justice Bruneau; but when the conservatives returned to power, he was not continued in this position. Besides his writings in *L'Avenir*, he occasionally contributed to the *Franco-Canadien* and also to *L'Ordre*, in which latter paper, he published several remarkable communications over the signature *Libéral mais Catholique*. As a writer, he was eloquent, correct and even dignified ; he also frequently indulged in verse. Mr. Dunn pays a high tribute to his religious and charitable character, and in an enthusiastic manner eulogizes his many and great abilities.

L'Hon. A. A. Dorion. Mr. Dunn gives a pithy sketch of this gentleman and his political career, in language at times severe and sarcastic. In fact he is far from being an admirer of M. Dorion's public life. This gentleman was born on the 17th January, 1818, at Ste. Anne de la Pérade, was educated at Nicolet and admitted to the bar in 1842. At this time, he sympathised with M. Papineau in his opposition to the union between Upper and Lower Canada, and was among the irreconcilable youths of that period. The revolution of 1848, in France, suggested to him the founding of a republic in this country, and in 1849, he published a manifesto to that end. With Papin and Daoust, he belonged to the *Club national démocratique.* Unlike others of the party, he was not violent, nor given to exaggerated language, but on the contrary, calm and polite. He was elected to the House of Assembly for Montreal, in 1854, and was immediately recognized as the chief of the liberal party ; but the author states that this distinction was due more to his personal dignity, courtesy and his persevering labor, than to his intellectual superiority over Laberge and Papin. The author deems it best to ignore his political career, his anti-Catholic votes, his project of annual parliaments and his proposal to make justices of the peace elective. In 1857, he refused to form a part of the conservative administration under Cartier, and in the following year was the chief of the short-lived Brown-Dorion cabinet. In 1861, he was defeated in Montreal by Cartier, and in 1862, he accepted a portfolio in the Macdonald-Sicotte ministry. Six months later, dissenting from his colleagues, nominally on the Intercolonial Railway question, he resigned. He subsequently became a member of the Macdonald-Dorion government, which was defeated in 1864. The author says, that the only important act of his political life was the appointment of M. Sicotte as judge, and that his public career was a failure. He did not carry the fire and energy, which characterized his pleadings at the Bar, into the House, and on its floor he was tame and timid. The people looked to him for new departures in politics and the inauguration of brilliant policies, but were disappointed. From the inception of Confederation, he has been the bitter opponent of the conservative party, and on the accession to power of the Liberals, he accepted office under the Mackenzie government, but retired from it, upon receiving the chief justiceship of the Superior Court. Mr. Dunn says he was a leader at the bar, but not in the House, and that as a judge he will be an honor to the bench.

Lucien Turcotte. This is a graceful tribute to a departed friend who, the author says, was as dear to him as a brother, and that their friendship was cemented during a period of mutual intercourse in Paris. His grief at M. Turcotte's death was rendered the more poignant, inasmuch as he was deprived, through unavoidable circumstances, of the melancholy satisfaction of tending his friend in his dying moments and hearing his parting words.

Lucien Turcotte was the third son of the late Hon. J. E. Turcotte, and at the same time his pupil, for it was from his father that he learnt, with infantile lips, the first lessons in the art of rhetoric, in which he afterwards so excelled. He was sent to Paris by the Laval University to complete his legal studies and on his return from Quebec, was appointed a professor at law in that institution. The author enthusiastically testifies to his abilities as a speaker and a writer, to his loving and sympathetic nature, and to his deeply religious and virtuous character. He died 12th January, 1874. These affecting pages are worthy of the author and his subject.

A propos du "Patois Canadien." This paper is on a theme to which Mr. Dunn has devoted much thought and research. He first remarks upon the very general ignorance, in France, respecting Canada, on the part of, in other respects, well informed men, travelers who have written miserable accounts of pretended experiences in this country. He denies the existence of a Canadian *patois*. He admits, however, that in the lower St. Lawrence the *habitants* mispronounce the *r*, and give the sound of *d* and *t* followed by *i* as if there was a *z* between them; for instance *dire* is pro: nced *dzire*, and *partir*, *partzir*. It is more the intonation that is at fault; in fact, the French spoken here is purer than that of the French peasant. The author, however, thinks the misfortune is, that his countrymen have not had the advantage of real French conversation, and, being mostly engaged in business and constantly obliged to speak English, fall into the habit of using the idioms of that language, not only in conversation, but in writing. Canadian journalism has been accused of being too much given to ideal speculation and theological discussions. Mr. Dunn, while asserting that the material progress of the country has not been neglected by its writers, does not endeavor to refute this accusation; but on the contrary, rather glories in the imputation, that, on a continent where every knee bends to the "almighty dollar" and where hard realities alone are appreciated, the French-Canadian press devotes some of its energies and abilities to the discussion of religious and philosophical subjects. It is a misfortune, he says, that here there is an utter absence of true criticism. Judgments are pronounced upon personal, or party considerations and not with regard to intrinsic merits, or faults. He concludes this well-penned article by quoting Paul-Louis-Courier, who says: "In France, there are five or six who know Greek, and fewer who know French;" the author adds,—and in Canada ! well, let us be satisfied that we do not speak a *patois.*" In strict truth Mr. Dunn could have affirmed that there are not more than five or six in Canada, who write French correctly; for but few have captured this fair and coy maiden and become her master.

Mr. Dunn has just rendered an important service to Canadian literature by the publication of a clear, methodical and etymological work, entitled *Glossaire Franco-Canadien.* It is evidently his aim, not only to show the historical development of the French language in this country, but even those irregularities and licenses *(locutions vicieuses)* indulged in by men, who pretend to be guides and controllers of modern style in literature. Mr. Dunn's guiding star is the preservation of the genius of *la langue Gauloise,* and such a transparent reflection of French thought and research, as will command the respect and improve the mind of every admirer of that literature.

The results of the introduction into our schools of Mr. Dunn's *Manuel de dessin industriel,* has been gratifying. In 1876, before they were in use, there were less than four hundred pupils taking lessons in linear drawing, but last year the number had increased to fifty thousand. These *Manuels,* with their accompanying series of geographical charts, are composed after the method of Walter Smith's system.

Mr. Dunn's qualities as a writer are clearness, precision

and purity of language. Kindly feeling animates his compositions, which attract attention by certain pleasing peculiarities. He has, moreover, the power of rendering abstruse subjects attractive, in particular those he prefers, by judiciously seasoning them with Gallic salt. In the *Pétition au Ministre de l'Instruction Publique*, he is eloquent, touching and persuasive. The author has somewhat adopted the style of the famous *Lettres d'un Vigneron*, by Paul-Louis-Courier, not unworthy of his model. From beginning to end, it is in the same affecting strain. To succeed in such a delineation of real hardship, a writer must be both sympathetic and forcible.

ARTHUR BUIES.

The name of Mr. Buies is well known to the reading community of this province. All admit that he is one of our most sparkling writers. His style is animated and happy, irradiated throughout by flashes of wit and humor. He has been called, by those who simply look upon the spicy side of character, the Henri Rochefort of Canada. Liberal in spirit and delighting in the literature of his country he has done his best to give practical evidence of these feelings and to increase its valuable store. To him, Mr. Hector Fabre and Carle-Tom (Mr. Gelinas) must be accorded the honor of being the only eminent *chroniqueurs* in the French language, of whom Canada can boast.

Le Saguenay et la Vallée du Lac St. Jean, by that gentleman has been published at an opportune moment, when the attention of all in the p.ovince of Quebec is directed towards this territory, which undoubtedly will be the future abode of many thousands of our countrymen.

Of this book, he, in his preface, expresses himself as follows : " We now present to the reader a work which shows its own fruit, the compiling of which has rendered it dear to us,—which we have tasted and loved, according as it imposed upon us fresh labors and its importance grew before our eyes,—a work, in fine, which we hope will benefit all who carefully study it and seek in it fidelity as to facts as well as descriptions, and a jealous care to neglect nothing that may answer in advance all enquiries which may be suggested to the mind."

In the beginning, Mr. Buies refers to the recent opening up of this too long unknown country, through which their burning zeal, when the greater part of America was still undiscovered, had led the pious and fervent missionaries of the olden time to face all difficulties and to tempt hidden dangers in order to make known the Christian faith to the savages of the forest. The love of adventure had drawn the plucky *coureurs de bois* also away from civilization into those mysterious regions. A well merited compliment is paid these zealous missionaries by the author in the succeeding lines : " Let us not forget them above all, these soldier apostles, who everywhere sought the most obscure retreats to offer up their lives. Let us not forget that their incessant labors, their extensive missions, recounted by them with a humility as great as their devotion, form the most complete history of an epoch, wherein courage, patience and a spirit of self-sacrifice were carried, as it were, beyond human endurance, and seemed as a daily repeated miracle in the precarious existence of our poor colony."

Mr. Buies gives details, referring to the different localities, in a comprehensive manner, as also a geographical description of the former and present districts of the Saguenay, furnishing the names, positions and boundaries of the different townships. I s description of the river Saguenay itself and its lofty and imposing rocky outlet, capes Eternity and Trinity, are an excellent specimen of word-painting. He gives a faithful and poetic idea of the famous echoes of the locality, so much admired by tourists and lovers of nature. Grande Baie, or Ha ! Ha ! Bay, he looks upon as the future commercial centre of the territory, and it will doubtless become so. Twenty-five rivers fall into the Saguenay, twelve of which are navigable by canoes, and two or three by vessels of small dimensions; some of these are famous as salmon rivers, among which may be mentioned the *Sainte-Marguerite.*

In 1828, when an official exploration of the country was made, Tadoussac contained not a dozen buildings. Mr. Buies gives its history from 1640, then under the Jesuit missionaries, supplying the names of the different fathers and priests, thence to 1863. In 1837, was formed a company of French-Canadians, to manufacture lumber in the Saguenay country, and, in the following season, a colony settled there and built saw-mills, selling the deals to the late Hon. Mr. Wm. Price. The latter eventually became proprietor of the whole establishment, which was greatly enlarge by him and his sons. A short sketch is given of the life and doings of a singular character, a

Scotch half-breed, Peter McLeod, who was at the same time, "as brave as a lion and gentle as a child." From church registers and census returns, Mr. Buies demonstrates the advancement of the country, especially of the townships of Chicoutimi, Saint Dominique, de Joachim, Normandin, Le Haut Saguenay, Labarre and Lake St. John, and the parishes south and west of that lake. Next follows a chapter, descriptive of the great tributaries of Lake St. John, among which he mentions Chamouchouane, Mistassini and Péribouca.

Chapter XII is very interesting and is devoted to the scenery and physical character of the Saguenay. It possesses not only a general, but a scientific interest; the geology, atmospheric effects, climatic influences, its fauna and flora being fully and attractively treated, and every natural object, worthy of attention, adequately depicted. The author advances the theory that at one time a great cataclysm rent and deluged the Saguenay region; mountains were cleft, torrents raged, vast rivers disappeared and new streams burst over virgin courses; the whole face of nature was violently changed, leaving the extraordinary features which this romantic district now presents. The exposition of this not improbable theory, calls forth a display of descriptive power which every man of sentiment and lover of nature must cordially admire.

In reference to the road between Quebec and Lake St. John, Mr. Buies tells us that it can be traversed, in winter, in a few days, but much remains to be done to render it practicable in summer. Important statistical information respecting public instruction throughout the rural parishes and municipalities is offered the reader.

A chapter on the railroad to Lake St. John relates the history of the enterprise to the present date, including the bill, presented by E. Beaudet, Esq., the energetic member for Chicoutimi, at the last session of the local legislature, the passage of which assured the success of the road.

This useful and important volume, which is illustrated with charming artotypes of the most important localities, closes with the history of the St. Lawrence Towboat company, and its large traffic with the Saguenay district.

The character of this book is of the practical kind, being mainly, as I have already stated, a record of historical, statistical and topographical facts, which may not be as attractive to the general reader as others of the author's works, such as his *Chroniques*; yet, its value to the historian and the friend of colonization can not be over valued. He has noted the phenomena of the great wave of immigration and acquainted the reader with the toils, hardships and successes of settlers. The life and general social experience of this class have been well described; Mr. Buies' relations and comments being marked by a sympathetic spirit, highly appreciative and creditable.

Few will gainsay the fact that Mr. Buies is one of our purest and most elegant writers in the French language, and that his diction is of the choicest. He does not, however, sustain this purity and elegance throughout all his works, and this *laissez aller* is not by any means confined to him, as has been frequently noticed in these reviews. His best compositions are certainly found in his earlier *Chroniques*, several of which are classical in style and original. A vein of satire runs through the best pages of his compositions, rendering their perusal entertaining and amusing.

JOSEPH MARMETTE.

The historical and romantic incidents of early Canadian life, the traditions of the dim but interesting past, have ever formed an attractive mine to the patriotic and antiquarian writer. There is nothing in recent events— the ordinary experience of a prosaic, practical age—to rival in charm and pathos the far-off experiences and scenes, religious and sentimental dreams, the struggles often too tragic, the hopes, toils and fears of the bold, adventurous men, who laid on the solid old rocks of the Laurentian Hills and plains the stable foundations of *La Nouvelle France*, the present great province of Quebec. Few French-Canadian prose-writers have sketched with more felicitous pen those remote events and scenes, which inspire at this day even foreign writers, than Mr. Marmette, the author of *Héroisme et Trahison*. In this volume, the writer has been happy in the choice and treatment of his subject.

Under the first heading, *Héroisme*, he describes the chivalrous defence of Fort Verchères, by Mlle. de Verchères, on the 22nd October, 1692, against a band of forty-five Indians, she having no other protection than her two brothers, under 12 years of age, one servant, two cowardly soldiers, an old man of eighty and some women and children, who, in their terror, embarrassed her with their screams and lamentations. With a sublime courage, equal to that of Jeanne d'Arc, she simulated with a like skill a state of preparation and confidence, which fortunately prevented any serious attack, till assistance arrived from Montreal. She is well described, not only as acting with extraordinary heroism within the little fort, but, though under fire of the enemy, as thrice making sorties; once to warn a party arriving in a boat by the river, again to secure some clothing, and once more for the protection of cattle in danger of falling into the hands of her vigilant foes. The act of this young girl, of barely fourteen years of age, whose splendid courage and fortitude have been fully recognized by even foreign authors (Parkman included), effectually checked the Iroquois, who on every occasion of success became emboldened and destructively aggressive. Mr. Marmette appends at the end of his book the memoir addressed by Mlle. de Verchères to his Majesty Louis XV., preserving all the peculiarities of style and composition of the original manuscript.

The author next relates some incidents which occurred at Quebec between 1755 and 1759, under the caption of *Traitres et Braves*. These are taken from his historical novel *L'Intendant Bigot*, the must popular and certainly the most dramatic of his four works. In the year 1755 a grievous famine raged, sweeping off large numbers of the poor, whilst the unscrupulous Bigot and his satellites were rioting in shameless profligacy. It is midnight of Christmas, when an old officer, M. de la Rochebrune, pinched with cold and hunger to the last degree, resolved to pawn his St. Louis cross of gold at the Intendant's palace stores. On the way thither, the officer and his young daughter, a lovely girl of fourteen are startled at the blaze of light illuminating the palace windows, during one of the Intendant's festivals. The pleasures of the evening are suddenly interrupted and shaded by the entry of the aged, suffering M. de la Rochebrune and his wan-visaged, but beautiful daughter. Words of galling truth are addressed to Bigot before his painted courtezans and his other depraved attendants, whose hearts are too hard and whose consciences too seared to be touched by either misery, or reproof; and the ruffian varlets eject both father and daughter to the furies of the midnight blast. The ball ended, Bigot leads Mme. de Péan to her vehicle, when she stumbles over an object which, when torches are brought, is found to be the corpse of the suppliant rebuker of a few hours previous, alongside of which lies the unconscious form of his daughter, half buried in the drifting snow. "*Mon Dieu*," exclaims Mme. de Péan, "*Je ne dormirai pas de la nuit, c'est bien sûr.*" This tragic event is narrated with thrilling effect, in the author's best style.

Chapter II. graphically describes a conflict between

the French and Indians, and outposts of Wolfe's army, before the battle of Beauport, the sacking and burning by the British of the villages on the north and south shores of the St. Lawrence and the Island of Orleans. Next is given the disclosures of a plot of Bigot's and his two associates, de Vergor and Sournois, to deliver Quebec into the hands of the English, to secure which they communicate with Wolfe and promise him an easy ascent to the Plains of Abraham. It is true that Bigot's character was vileness and wickedness itself, but it is doubtful if it be laden with the weight of this treachery, which may be assumed, of course, by the novelist for dramatic purposes. He was, doubtless, equal to such a crime, but the high character of Wolfe would probably form an insuperable barrier to its perpetration. An account of the battle of the Plains is written in a spirited manner. The author has here also taken the novelist's licence in reference to the number of combatants engaged, giving the majority to the English, whilst the official statement proves the contrary; he further makes out the battle to have been long contested, whereas it is generally admitted that but a few minutes elapsed from the first encounter when the French ranks broke and fled. The concluding chapter is devoted to the punishment of the wretched Bigot and his accomplices. This little book forms a creditable contribution to Canadian literature, of which its author may be proud.

Le Tomahawk et L'Epée, also by Mr. Marmette, is a

series of historical anecdotes, taken from two of his works, *Le Chevalier de Mornac*, published in 1873, and *François de Bienville*, in 1870. In this volume he treats principally of the hostilities and their savage character between the French and the Iroquois, previous to the arrival of the famous Carignan regiment in 1665. In Le Chevalier de Mornac, he has succeeded in typifying the *gentilhomme gascon*, daring, courageous, and poor, but generous to a fault. The first incident has for subject, *La dispersion des Hurons*. It is supposed to be related in 1664, in the house of Mme. Guillot at St. Thomas, Quebec, by *Renard Noir*, a Huron chief, to the hostess, Mlle Richecourt, and her cousin, le Chevalier de Mornac. The sky was radiant with the aurora borealis, an account of which is given, and also of the terrible earthquakes of the year previous, recorded in *Les Relations des Jésuites*, which were preceded by the same resplendent phenomena. *Renard Noir* relates that he had joined Champlain when a young chief, and had learned from him, not only the art of war, but various useful accomplishments, and had been converted to Christianity. He tells how he and several others of his tribe were, when near Three Rivers, attacked by their enemies, the Iroquois, whom they defeated after a severe struggle. On the return to the village to reap the reward of victory, they were met by an old man, an inhabitant of it, who transformed their delight into utter wretchedness by the announcement that their village had been assailed by another Iroquois party, and all their squaws, children, and old men massacred, or captured. *Renard Noir* also narrates with touching pathos the annihilation, almost, of his tribe at Fort St. Louis, and its dispersion later, throughout the length and breadth of the land. The Indian paints his scenes in the quaint, expressive language of his race, which heightens the dramatic effect of the narrative.

On the 30th June, 1665, the Marquis de Tracey arrived at Quebec as Viceroy of New France, to the great satisfaction and amid the rejoicings of the inhabitants, for several companies (some historians say twenty-four, I believe) of the expected Carignan regiment had arrived. Mr. Marmette's descriptive talents do justice to the grand display of feudal pomp and dignity, which marked the progress of the Marquis and his *cortège* from the landing to the Château St. Louis. Four companies of the Carignan regiment were immediately despatched up the St. Lawrence to build forts on the River Richelieu and elsewhere, to prevent the depredations of the Iroquois. When the Richelieu fort was about completed, a midnight attack was made upon it by *Griffe d'Ours* and his band, who were repulsed, and himself taken a prisoner. Notwithstanding the request of the commanding officer, the Indians, friendly to the French, proceeded to torture *Griffe d'Ours* in the most ingeniously cruel manner. Among the most eager for this inhuman abuse of power was

Renard Noir, whose squaw, in the attack upon the village, *Griffe d'Ours* had murdered and scalped. At this moment *Renard Noir* is in a dying condition from wounds received during the attempt upon the fort, but, still bent upon revenge, crawls towards *Griffe d'Ours*, and by a superhuman effort gathers sufficient strength to scalp his enemy, and then falls back exhausted. The torturing of *Griffe d'Ours* now begins in earnest; they cut out pieces of his flesh and apply red hot coals to his wounds, whilst their victim smiles derisively and goads them on by reminding them, how much better he had succeeded in similar cruelties practiced upon their people. He is tied to a post and the funeral pile set fire to; the binding cords are burnt and *Griffe d'Ours* falls into the flames, but suddenly rises with a firebrand in each hand and hurls them in the midst of his enemies. A struggle follows and he is overpowered; they cut off his feet and hands and pitch his trunk back into the flames. For an instant he does not move:—" *Mais tout à coup, ô horreur! on vit ce corps mutilé, déchiré, brûlé, s'agiter encore, se rouler sur lui-même et se soulever à demi sur ces tisons ardents, et là, montrant à nû son crâne sanglant, ses membres incrustés de cendres chaudes et de charbons ardents qui sifflaient au contact du sang, il se traîna dans les flammes et cracha une dernière insulte à ses bourreaux interdits.*" The enactment of this frightful scene is similar to one witnessed by Père Jérôme Lalemant. It is one of the most revolting incidents of the Indian warfare of that time, and affords the author a well used opportunity for the display of his descriptive powers, and is depicted in a manner painfully graphic.

The first novel Mr. Marmette published was *François de Bienville*, which established his reputation as a conscientious and faithful portrayer of the social customs and habits of *La Nouvelle France* of the seventeenth century. It abounds in true and careful descriptions of Quebec of that day, and of the trials of the people of the period. The love passages of the novel, which are treated with delicacy of feeling, relieve the narration of the tragical events of the historical drama.

In *L'Epée* there is an account of the second siege of Quebec and other *tableaux historiques*, extracted from the above novel. It opens with the arrival at the capital of the Count de Frontenac, the then Governor. The author gives particulars of a bill of fare of those days in the Château St. Louis, and the nature of the different dishes served. Phipps had destroyed *Port Royal* on his way to Quebec, and he now imperiously summons the Count to surrender the city. It is graphically told how the messenger was received, blindfolded, and deceived as to the state of the stronghold, and the haughty reply of the Governor: "I will answer your general only by the mouths of my cannon, that he may learn that a man like me is not to be summoned after this fashion. Let him do his best and I will do mine." The exchange of cannonades, the capture of an English flag by two Canadians, named D'Orsy Bienville and Clermont, and the bombardment, are all cleverly witten, as also the defeat of the English at Beauport. Phipps is at last compelled to raise the siege and sail for Boston. A few hours after his departure, he had the misfortune of losing several vessels, completing his discomfiture and humiliation.

La Mort d'un Brave relates the surrounding by a body of Canadians under François de Bienville, who was second in command to de Vaudreuil, at Repentigny, of a band of Iroquois, who had taken refuge in a house. The latter have the advantage of cover, and the assailants decide to storm the building, in which was the chief *Dent de Loup*, the *ennemi acharné* of *Bras de fer*, who was among the attacking party. Bienville, the fearless, with axe in hand, rushes to the door to break it open; but *Dent de Loup* from the cellar shoots him down, and he is borne to shelter by *Bras de fer*. As he peacefully passes away, giving advice to his brother and sending farewell messages to his mother, the fierce howls and death song of the perishing Iroquois are heard from the burning house, amid the crackling of the flames and the fall of its timbers.

Les Macchabées de la Nouvelle France is dedicated by Mr. Marmette to his father, a well educated and noble-hearted physician, residing at St. Thomas, Quebec. This is a purely historical study of an important period in the annals of this country, and relates the history of the Canadian family Le Moyne, from 1641 to 1763. Charles Le Moyne, for several encounters with the Indians and their defeat, and for successful peace negotiations, received from the Crown the *fief de Longueuil*, opposite Montreal, besides large money grants. The Hudson Bay expedition of d'Iberville and de Sévigny was crowned with success, reaping high honors for the daring brothers; while de Maricourt proved victorious in many skirmishes with the Iroquois in and around Montreal. Again, de Maricourt and d'Iberville's campaigns in Newfoundland were a series of brilliant achievements, and d'Iberville carried terror to the English in the far-off settlements of Hudson Bay. The latter was also one of the discoverers of the mouths of the Mississippi, and made valuable researches in that then unknown region. De Sévigny had the honor of driving the Spanish from Florida, whilst de Bienville founded New Orleans. The above are a few of the important services rendered by this valiant family, not only to France, but to the world. On the ocean and in the pathless forest, these brave men were equally at home, achieving success and crowning themselves with glory; some of them dying in the hour of victory and the heyday of life, whilst others reached a ripe old age, laden with honors and renown. The author had good scope for description in the voyages of his heroes from the glacial borders of Hudson Bay to the sunny shores of the Gulf of

Mexico, and he made capital use of his opportunities. This family was deserving of having their deeds recorded in the world's history, and Mr. Marmette's able sketch will materially assist in spreading their fame.

Two of the novels above referred to, *François de Bienville* and *Le Chevalier de Mornac* have been dramatized and placed upon our Quebec boards on several occasions before delighted and enthusiastic audiences. Last winter he composed a comedy based upon social episodes entitled : "*Il ne faut désespérer de rien*," which was also a decided success, and critics on that occasion spoke of it in the highest terms. Mr. Marmette is presently engaged in writing a work treating of our social traits, peculiarities and customs, "*A travers la vie;*" the first chapter of which appeared in a new review, "*La Nouvelle France*," under the able management of Mr. Jacques Auger, which promises to be the most important in the French language in the country. Judging by this first instalment, I would say that it will be Mr. Marmette's master-piece.

This author's works maintain their interest throughout. He recalls the distant past by a vivid imagination, appearing as an actor himself in the stormy scenes, by the force of his sympathy and word-painting. One enjoys, in his writings, not only the pleasures of romance, but the valuable information of history. The old Canadians revive under his pen and appear to us in their quaint, homely costumes, their simple, social, and gallant characters, and interesting habits and customs. His stories, in their subjects, style and spirit, breathe the odour of chivalry, while the reader can fancy himself within the sound of martial music and the clash of hostile arms. The adventures of the old *coureurs des bois* are vividly told, the descriptions of Canadian scenery by flood and field, of dangers heroically faced. of heart-rending scenes evince lively powers of fancy and delineation, forcibly proving that the author has made his native land, its history and characteristics his favorite study.

Mr. Marmette perhaps makes too free use of adjectives, but this is a fault that few authors have avoided in their earlier literary efforts. However, it is but just to add that in his later publications, which I have read, I have noticed a great improvement in this and in a few other details. In dialogue, the stumbling block of so many writers, he excels; and in other respects he is deserving of high encomium.

NAPOLÉON LEGENDRE.

A mes Enfants, by this gentleman, are short tales, whose object is to elevate the youthful, by instilling into them pure and good thoughts, and show a knowledge of the heart and a power of interest particularly befitting his purpose. Generous and noble actions are presented in an attractive guise that cannot fail to please.

One story, *L'Encan*, a sale by authority of justice, is a tale of misery, the like of which is too often witnessed. It is worthy óf reproduction and of occupying a conspicuous place in *Le Magazin de l'Éducation d'Hetzel de Paris*, which is the *ne plus ultra* of such periodicals. Interspersed with the narratives are short poems, which might be called hymns, and are worthy of being attentively read. Few books are better calculated to warn children against evil and encourage them to good than this; its spirit, even in warning, being kindly, cheering and persuasive. Mr. Legendre does not pretend to paint model children, who, he says, and with truth, are generally failures. He depicts the characteristic idiosyncrasies and precocities of children, which appear in them so interesting and captivating, and often verify the old adage, "the child is father to the man."

In *Le collier bleu de Mariette*, the author brings to

light a hidden fault in a young child, who was really not given to its commission and she is rebuked for it, but methinks the remedy was severe and the punishment too humiliating. In fact there is also a stain of duplicity in the apparently effusive behavior of the parents which was to end in cruel exposure, but doubtless the author believes in the old axiom, "*aux grands maux les grands remèdes.*"

Mr. Legendre is certainly an accurate writer and *par excellence* the narrator of children's stories. There are passages in this little book that must set vibrating in the soul of every parent sympathetic chords, and in every child a spirit of emulation. Mr. Legendre is also a poet and has written charming effusions, more graceful however than forcible. One of his pieces has pleased me greatly, a poetic rendering of the Lord's prayer, entitled *Le soir*, which is admirable and will find a prominent and lasting place in our literature.

BENJAMIN SULTE.

Au coin du feu, by this author, is a very readable work of history and fancy. The first sketch describes the *Pélissier* cavern, in the township of Wakefield, county of Ottawa, in the Laurentian range, which contains six or seven rude caverns or grottoes; there are twenty-two or twenty-three in other parts of the country. The *Pélissier*, named after its discoverer, is the most wonderful, extending six hundred feet into the bowels of the earth, with a descent of one hundred and fifty feet. The grottoes are as white as snow and resemble polished marble, with grey corridors, black walls and drab alcoves; presenting a perfect combination of colors. In other parts are visible white quartz and ferruginous stones, which brilliantly scintillate in torch-light. No vestige of vegetation, not even moss, is to be seen in these arid chambers. At the further end, by a ladder, a lower story or chamber is reached, containing a rock-imitation of a seat, on which sat Lady Dufferin during a visit she made to this weird region. The cavern is supposed to have formed a portion of the channel or outlet of a lake in the immediate neighborhood, and many believe there is a subterranean one beneath.

Une Chasse à l'ours and *Le Loup-Garou*, are sketches of bush life, evidently by an experienced bush-ranger.

The bear and *loup-garou* appear only in fancy to draw out the author's humor.

The historical papers, *Jean Nicolet* and *Iroquois et Algonquins*, evince much research. The first in rendering justice to one of the most intrepid pioneers and travelers, and the second in tracing the tangled historical shreds of the two Indian nations more immediately connected with Canada. The latter especially is interesting reading.

Le Canada en Europe is a clever *exposé* of the ignorance displayed by English and French, in general, touching matters Canadian. The mistakes committed by those otherwise well informed, on this subject, are certainly amusing. He states that prominent London journalists, who are supposed never to make mistakes, can not tell whether Canada forms part of the Cape of Good Hope or the Argentine Republic. M. Gustave Aimard, one of the best portrayers of Indian life in America, when speaking of Canada, says, "that it has a population of twenty-five thousand, but could contain six times that number." The author makes the calculation, 150,000; which is about the population of Montreal. Six years ago, a despatch from Downing street requested the Governor General to immediately forward arms and military stores to British Columbia by land, instead of by water! A post office clerk, in France, when given a letter to post to Quebec, asked whether it should be sent *via* Panama, or

Cape Horn! It appears that one of the impressions prevailing among a number in France and England, is that " French Canadians are in the habit of taking squaws for wives!" It was only the other day that the *Figaro* of Paris, stated that "Mlle. Lajeunesse *(Albani)* is of French extraction, although *(quoique)* born at Mon'real." The author adds, "*ce 'quoique' est à croquer.*" Anthony Trollope, twenty years ago, wrote that "at Montreal and Quebec, the French Canadians are all water carriers and sawyers of wood." I may mention myself, the fact that the English government long annually sent out a flag-post for the citadel of Quebec, which probably had been grown in Canadian forests. I have heard it related by a lady that when traveling in Ireland, she was asked by a professor of Trinity College, Dublin, whether she was really a native of Canada, and on being assured that such was the case, he expressed his astonishment that " she was so fair;" and his air did not suggest the slightest flavor of " blarney." Many will recall the ludicrous statements, as to Canadian geography, made by certain English statesmen, in the Commons, during the Trent affair; one declared that Canada was separated from the United States by the Isthmus of Panama.

Mr. Sulte is severe in his reproaches against France for the neglect of her *quondam* colony. The last provincial loan obtained, through the skilful financing of the Hon. J. A. Chapleau, from France, and the operation of the

Crédit Foncier (a sequel to the policy of the Premier) will assuredly bring about relations between the two countries, most advantageous to both. Other indications in the same direction are various industries started by French capitalists in different parts of the province; all of which must be gratifying to the author as they are to the public generally.

The book closes with an amusing sketch of the wonder and even terror produced on the inhabitants of an out-of-the-way French Canadian village, by the ear-piercing shriek of a steamboat whistle, and an inquiry into the history of the brass cannon, found in 1826, on a sand bank, opposite Champlain, in the St. Lawrence.

Mr. Sulte is one of the most versatile of French-Canadian writers and has dealt with many subjects, relating to Canada; history, voyages, essays, reviews, sketches, ballads and sonnets have been alternately his themes. In prose and poetry he is equally at home; no one, however, can be *facile princeps* in so many branches, and he forms no exception to this rule. In matters referring to the history of *La Nouvelle France*, he is thoroughly *au fait*, and they are generally treated in a pleasing and graceful manner. He has written some excellent things, especially in poetry, but his diction, at times, might be purer.

LOUIS-P. TURCOTTE.

A perusal of *Le Canada sous l'Union*, 1841—1867, by Mr. Turcotte produces a strong feeling of regret that the author, a young man of true literary taste, and of intellectual gifts and painstaking disposition did not longer live to further enrich Canadian literature. His aim was to give a correct and impartial *résumé* of the history of Upper and Lower Canada of this period. In the introduction is an excellent epitome of the history of Canada from 1608—the year of the foundation of the city of Quebec by Champlain—to 1840, that of the union of the two Canadas. Without endorsing all the opinions of the author, it is but fair that I should mention some of them in illustration of the tenor of his thoughts and the scope of his work.

Mr. Turcotte accuses the first governor, after the union, Lord Sydenham, of an anglicizing and protestantizing spirit, adding that when his death at Kingston left the office to Sir Charles Bagot, that gentleman showed himself honest and well-intentioned. Unfortunately he was trammelled by a weak coalition cabinet, but strove to carry out the intention of the English government, and modify the laws so unjust and oppressive to the French Canadians, who had reason to complain of the usurpations of the English minority, especially represented by the "Family Compact." This government collapsing was succeeded by the LaFontaine-Baldwin coalition, which heartily assisted Sir Charles in abolishing or amending the objectionable statutes. It was under this administration the American Boundary question was settled, so much to the disadvantage of England and Canada—a bad precedent too often followed since, as history testifies. The death of Sir Charles Bagot, in 1843, was deeply regretted by the Canadians. He was succeeded by Lord Metcalfe, when Montreal became the capital. A difficulty between him and his ministers, with regard to the exercise of patronage, brought about their resignation, when the Viger-Draper cabinet was formed. Lord Metcalfe is described as liberal and just to all races and parties. His successor, Lord Cathcart, the then commandant of the English forces in Canada, was appointed in 1845; it being deemed advisable to have a military governor on account of the troubles then existing between the mother country and the United States. Under him the militia was organized and brought to a fair state of efficiency. Mr. Turcotte expresses admiration of Lord Cathcart's administration. Lord Elgin was the next Governor-General, his advisers being the Sherwood Daly cabinet, succeeded by that of the LaFontaine-Baldwin, when the use of the French language in parliamentary debate was again sanctioned. The indemnification, or rebellion losses controversy is clearly noticed, and also the difficulties which marked its sanction by His Excellency, including the riots and the burning of the parliament buildings in Montreal, with the splendid library and important public documents contained in it— a loss exceeding $400,000. Lord Elgin's administration is not unreasonably described as the most important under the Union, not only on account of the gravity of the measures passed, but of the simultaneous progress of the country. The public revenue had risen from one to four million dollars. Reciprocity with the United States was obtained and the settlement of the wild lands greatly extended. The population rose to two millions, and the national credit stood high. In 1854, Sir Edmund Head succeeded Lord Elgin, his advisers being the McNab-Taché administration, which soon dissolved, owing to jealousies between its Upper and Lower Canadian members. Sir Edmund Head, requested Colonel Taché to form a new cabinet, an honor well deserved, as the colonel's high principles entitled him to every confidence ; his views were broad and enlightened ; his parliamentary experience extensive and varied and his probity above suspicion. The measures of the Taché-Macdonald Ministry were important, including the codification of the civil laws of Lower Canada, the Judicial Decentralization Act, reforms in the administration of Justice, prison and asylum management, the making of the Legislative Council elective, acts for the promotion of education, colonization, and the encouragement of trade and agriculture. In 1855, Mr. Chauveau succeeded the veteran Dr. Meilleur, as Superintendent of Education, whose valuable services therein can not be over-estimated. The author highly praises Mr. Chauveau's administration of this department, crediting him with numerous useful reforms. In 1866, after Her Majesty's decision, the government was removed to Ottawa, the selection of which was a surprise to many public men, and I may add, has been since regretted by all parties. In 1857, Colonel Taché abandoned political life for needful rest after having served his country during ten consecutive years in various official positions of the highest importance, and was regretted by the leaders of both shades of politics. Shortly after his retirement, in acknowledgment of his public services, he was knighted. A short review of the literature and *beauxarts* of that period is here given. The Macdonald-Cartier cabinet was the next formed, a few years after which the liberals obtained office and remained in power but a few hours, when the Cartier-Macdonald cabinet was formed. The administration of Sir Edmund Head, though not in all respects happy or popular, particularly with the people of Upper Canada, was yet characterized by a pretty rapid growth and development of both provinces. He was succeeded by Lord Monk, in whose term the American civil war broke out and the Trent difficulty occurred, nearly leading to hostilities between England and the

United States. Great patriotism was manifested on that occasion and he specifies particularly the French Canadians who again gave proof of their fidelity and attachment to the British Crown. In 1864, the Macdonald-Dorion cabinet was obliged to resign through insufficient support, when Sir Etienne Taché was summoned by Lord Monk to form a ministry. He accepted the task with great reluctance, feeling that his health was not equal to the strain and excitement of political life, but his patriotism overcame these objections. At the next session the Taché-Macdonald government was defeated, and the Taché-Macdonald & Brown coalition came into existence. In 1864, Sir Louis H. LaFontaine died, an eminent statesman and distinguished jurisconsult, and on the 20th July 1865, followed him, Sir Etienne Taché, universally lamented as an eminent patriot. Many believe that his death was hastened by the cares and anxieties of office, at a time when his health required absolute rest and abstention from all excitement. Mr. Turcotte says that this noble gentleman had completed a brilliant career, having received the highest honors from the Crown, been twice chief of cabinets, knighted by his Sovereign, and elected President of the Confederation Convention at Quebec. His funeral took place at Montmagny with great solemnity and pomp, and was attended by his colleagues, by eminent statesmen, judges, military officers and the dignitaries of the church. Sir Narcisse Belleau was the next premier. Meantime Confederation had been agreed upon and adopted by the Legislatures of Ontario, Quebec, New Brunswick and Nova Scotia,—when a new era dawned on Canada. With truth the writer concludes : " Notwithstanding countless, bitter political struggles, the union of the Canadas resulted in the formation, in the space of fourteen years, out of two provinces dissatisfied and sparsely populated, into one, prosperous, populous, independent and satisfied."

Mr. Turcotte has supplied our youth with a valuable text book, exhibiting industry and research in the amount and arrangement of its information. He treats the acts and policy of the ministers of both parties with fairness and candor, giving credit for success and noticing impartially failures and mistakes of whatever party. His object appeared that of an honest and faithful historian, endeavoring to do justice to all alike. He ever remembered he was a French-Canadian, priding himself in the progress of his race, particularly in its courageous and determined efforts to secure its full and just rights ; the amplest rights of British subjects, whether in remote colonies or on the free soil of Great Britain. *L'Histoire du Canada*, by L'Abbé Ferland, *L'Histoire de Cinquante ans*, by M. Bédard, and *Le Canada sous l'Union* form a complete trilogy of the history of Canada, beginning in the dim past, to the era of Confederation. Sir Francis Hincks did the author the honor of proposing to translate his work into English, but he feared that its publication might endanger his position as an employé in the civil service; for, to certain passages some political partizans had taken umbrage. For my own part I must say, in all honesty, that I have failed to find in them anything blameworthy; on the contrary, as I have already said, he is just, impartial and dispassionate. In reference to the work itself, it might have been more carefully written, and betrays the youth and want of experience of the author. His premature death i͇ the more to be regretted, since he might have in a new edition expunged such errors and given greater vigor, nerve and consistency to his style.

PAUL De CAZES.

For some years, Canada had the advantage of being represented in France by a gentleman who, during that time, proclaimed the advantages and resources of Canada by his diplomatic skill and in a series of able articles, which appeared in *Le Monde* of Paris, and other journals of the same high standing. In this Mr. de Cazes not only carried out the obligations of his official duties, but followed the dictates and sentiments of his patriotism. He sought, on every occasion, to make the climatic and general physical advantages of Canada, his adopted country, widely known throughout Europe, and to correct the false impressions there existing, namely, that we had no literature, no history, no reputation. Besides disseminating facts in regard to our resources, financial prosperity and growing importance, he commented upon the excellence and high standard of our educational system and the ability and cleverness of our authors; their style and characteristic traits of composition being brought out in an able manner. He made every effort to acquaint the literary and reading public of Europe with the fact that in Canada, as in France itself, no work regardless of truth, or of the purest taste, would receive any countenance, and that not only national but literary pride controlled every thinker on social, historical and political subjects in *La Nouvelle France*. The contributions of Mr. de Cazes excited a great deal of attention at the time, and elicited most favorable comments. No one, who can estimate the merits of good French composition, can possibly overlook his writings—they exhibit a lucid, plain and logical style in conception, whose greater proportion reflects the earliest history of this country with fair impartiality; while his criticisms upon the literary labors of compatriots are distinguished by justice and friendly interest. Those who visited Paris, while Mr. de Cazes was the representative of our Government, can not soon forget his courtesy and urbanity.

At the time of the Paris exhibition, this gentleman wrote a work, entitled *Notes sur le Canada*, a second edition of which, with much additional and valuable information, I now review.

It is not every day that one is privileged to read a book, containing such an amount of interesting and important matter within so small a compass. Its facts must represent the essence of many volumes carefully digested; and yet this condensation does not affect the ease and grace of style, for which the writer is famed, both here and abroad. Its characteristics include lucidity, aptness of expression and felicity of illustration. The matter is not sacrificed to the style, nor the latter to the former. *Multum in parvo* has been the author's guiding rule; a rule which can not be too rigidly followed by youthful *littérateurs*, or contributors to the press.

In a few short pages, Mr. de Cazes gives an able summary of the events connected with Confederation; after which he treats of our climate, sanitary circumstances, increase of population, vast wealth of fuel of the best kinds, mines, agriculture, manufactures, forests and fisheries. The second chapter is a clever *résumé* of Canadian history under French rule, ending with the battle on the Plains. In reference to the numbers of men engaged on both sides in that celebrated encounter, he like Mr. Marmette places the numerical advantage on the side of the English. He also states that victory was long undecided, whereas as I have already mentioned, it is generally admitted that within a few minutes of the general attack the French were defeated. Then follows an account of the British domination. He concludes with the remark, which is worthy of reproduction here:— "*Qu'aucun peuple au monde ne possède de plus grandes libertés politiques et religieuses.*"

Chapter III. deals with our natural and industrial products, and is replete with interesting details to the student of political economy. Mr. de Cazes fears that the Canadian farmers are affected with a leaning towards luxury, and instances proofs in support of his assertion. All hope that his prediction of a great industrial future for Canada will be realized. In the chapter, entitled

Commerce International, are given the tables of imports and exports from 1875 to 1879, inclusive. From them is argued a steady progress, notwithstanding the disastrous year of 1875, which he attributes to the financial crisis in the United States and the overstocking of the markets with all kinds of goods. He also refers to the increasing trade with France, and claims that many of the entries credited to England should go to France—the former acting as middlemen, at an expense to Canada that might be avoided, by importing direct. The figures of the trade between France and Canada show a steady improvement since 1874. The fact is recognized that Canada ranks fourth in the list of maritime nations. The author takes the Canadian census of 1865 and 1871 for comparison, showing that Canada stands favorably with the United States. The numbers of Catholics and Protestants, English and French, in Quebec and Ontario, are compared with interesting results. Of the Indian population, but 29,827 remain in Canada of the 190,000 of the time of the colonization by France.

In regard to education in this province, Mr. de Cazes alludes to the flattering mention M. Lavasseur made in his report of 1875 to the Academy of Moral and Political Sciences, and quotes, from the report of Hon. Mr. Ouïmet, the statement that Quebec was awarded at the Paris Exhibition four diplomas, four bronze medals, and four honorary distinctions for possessing "one of the most perfect systems of primary instruction." This must have been very gratifying to the superintendent for his conscientious and painstaking efforts on behalf of this good cause. The author gives an exhaustive report of the system of education in force here, and a great deal of statistical information in regard thereto and also lengthy extracts from the reports of the two gentlemen who have latterly had the direction of the Department of Public Instruction in this province, M.M. Chauveau and Ouimet. Mr. de Cazes traces the history of education from 1616 to the present time. He states, that the progress of elementary education was very slow until 1836, when the primary schools in actual operation numbered only 1,321, and the pupils in attendance, about 36,000 ; but soon afterwards, however, several colleges were established, which have since become important educational institutions, and these, combined with the efforts and zeal of the clergy and of certain members of the laity, gave a fresh impetus in the right direction. He mentions among the last, and "as in the first rank, Mr. Joseph François Perrault, the then prothonotary of Quebec and an ex-member of parliament, who devoted his leisure hours and his means to that eminently patriotic object of fostering and developing education in this country."

Mr. de Cazes, in continuing the history of education, gives other important and interesting details. He pronounces a high eulogium on the course adopted by the government to promote its advancement and dissemination. The state of education in the other provinces is enquired into and their statistics given. In fact, Mr. de Cazes has written an able epitome of the scholastic institutions of the provinces of Quebec, Ontario, New Brunswick, Nova Scotia, Prince Edward Island, Manitoba and British Columbia, which will be of great service to those seeking information on this important subject. In proportion to the population of Quebec, the school attendance on the part of children is 1 to 5·5 inhabitants; in Ontario, 1 to 3·5; in New Brunswick, 1 to 9·9; in Nova Scotia, 1 to 3·09. The author holds, on the question of immigration, that it benefits both countries affected; but little was done by Canada to promote it until 1870. Still, it may be remembered that Messrs. McGee and McDougall were Emigration Ministers before that time, and agents were sent to Ireland and England, and money voted to secure this object. The book closes with tables of nationality and religion, and valuable information in reference to postal matters.

There is only one thing wanting in connection with this attractive volume—the map which accompanied the first edition; always of great assistance to strangers. But in every other respect it is an improvement upon the latter, and shows on the part of the author much persevering labor and valuable research, with results creditable to his feelings towards this country, and his industry and intelligence. His style, I have already said, merits particular commendation, forming an additional attraction of the work.

JOSEPH TASSÉ

Les Canadiens de l'Ouest, by Mr. Tassé, is the result of ten years of labor and research, respecting the settlement and civilization of the Great West. The book (two volumes), will be most useful to students and untraveled readers generally, and to historians and writers of romance will present a rich harvest of episodes an' incidents of a varied and d amatic character. It, everywhere, gives creditable evidence of conscientious and careful work in compiling the biographies of the hardy French pioneers, who first explored and settled the western wilds. In these lives and narratives will be found exciting pictures of undaunted courage, ardent toil, plucky enterprise and successful achievements, of which Canadians may well be proud. Not a few of these scenes of struggle and labor of these intrepid pioneers are now great cities and thriving towns; the tangled wilderness and lonely plains, once the home only of the savage, the bear, the wolf, and the buffalo, being transformed into pleasant homesteads, farms and orchards, where happy thousands live in comfort and contentment. Portraits of some of the best known explorers illustrate these volumes, whose contribution to our early history will be read with profit and pleasure.

The index is carefully compiled and will be of great utility to the reader and student. In the narration of events and delineation of character, Mr. Tassé is very particular, and his facts, as to costumes, habits, etc., are reliable. His style may here and there lack warmth of color and animation, making a few of the relations appear somewhat monotonous, but he generally writes in neat phraseology, is happy in his descriptions and unaffected in his pathetic narration.

LA LITTÉRATURE CANADIENNE.

Under the above caption two volumes are published. The first contains a selection from newspapers and periodicals; learned lectures, airy sketches and entertaining essays which are presented in a convenient form for the improvement and amusement of the reader. The design of the work is highly commendable, for the productions of many of our literary men and able journalists are lost through not being published in a more durable shape than the columns of a newspaper or magazine. In this well arranged literary scrap book will be found information, thoughts and reflections well worthy of preservation and which will, no doubt, often delight the reader.

The first four papers in the first volume are from the pen of Mr. Etienne Parent who was long known as the veteran of the French-Canadian press, and during his journalistic career did effective service in the cause of popular rights and liberties. The earliest treatises on philosophy and political economy of this country were from his pen. Desirous of reaching to the roots of all social and political questions, he did his best but in language not always clear. Of the orthodox school of faith and philosophy and opposed to revolutionary or heterodox opinio.is, he, however, could recognize the close and natural connection between the most earnest faith in Providence and a system of belief in the physical conditions and relations of the universe, such as the orthodox thinkers and the ablest men have ever acknowledged. His friends assert that his object was not simply the exposition of modern philosophical innovations, but a desire to establish the true principles of faith and morality, upon which the highest interests of society depend. He was never hostile to the promulgation of new ideas or theories for the mere love of opposition, but gave them his full and fair consideration before expressing a definite judgment. His grand principle seemed to be, " truth first and for its own sake;" and if any social, or religious, system could not stand the crucial test of truthful and logical examination, he abandoned it at once, trusting to the Divine operations, which are ultimately destined to secure the regeneration and perfection of our race.

De l'importance et des devoirs du Commerce. Mr. Parent at the outset of his lecture delivered in 1852 traces the beginnings of commerce and trade, and its gradual growth and extension to the most distant countries, to the benefit of each. Thus commerce seeking new markets, gave an impetus to the discovery of strange and uninhabited lands, which were brought within the range of civilization, and in time developed. Thus it also led to the unravelling of the secrets of nature, arts and sciences, ever marching onwards to renewed efforts and achievements ; inventions abolishing space and time have been reached and new worlds opened up and barbarism greatly diminished ; education and industry, leading to luxury have been advanced, which may yet bring about the fraternization of all nations. Thus also commerce became a great agency of peace suggesting mediation, in national disputes. Napoleon I. called the English "a nation of shop-keepers," and yet it was this nation alone which could curb his ambition and exile him to an island prison. Mr. Parent dwells upon the noble career and duties of a merchant and points out the broad field of action before him. He says, that the countless cargoes of precious metals which were brought in galleons from Mexico and Peru to Spain, after the discovery of America, did not remain in that country, but found their way to England and France, in the purchase of goods which it was unable to produce, thus enriching the former countries while it was a continual drain upon the latter, which resulted in Spain becoming from the greatest in the world only a third rate power. How different was the fate of England ! She, too, lost her colonies, but instead of weakening her, this loss became a gain, through her commerce. Although a free-trader, he thinks in a young country, where capital and experience are wanting, some protection in the beginning should be given to our manufactures. This is the N. P. of the Conservative party of the year 1880. In Quebec, public spirit and commercial education are needed, and he recommends the study of the English and French languages, arithmetic, modern history and geography, political economy and book-keeping, to form men, able and worthy of conducting the commerce of the country and of reaping its many advantages.

Considérations sur le sort des classes ouvrières, is the subject of a lecture given by the same gentleman, in St. Roch, 15th April, 1852. He begins by contrasting the lot of the workingmen in this country, where some are able to indulge even in luxuries, with that of their brethren in Europe, who gain but a precarious livelihood and are often exposed to the greatest misery, whilst morally regardless of authority and without religion. These evils, he thinks, are caused by errors of government, errors of employers and errors of the workingmen themselves. In order to remedy them, sociability should be encouraged so as to create an interchange of thought and ideas and to give an impetus to education. Of all sins the author looks upon laziness as the worst. Strikes are condemned and the principles of political economy extolled. The same law which protects the master protects the servant, for competition is sure to find the true level of remuneration.

Mr. Parent would doubtless have condemned the excesses of some trade combinations, in this city, which have acted to their own detriment and the injury of the trade of our port. He recommends that a certain percentage of the wages' fund, be deposited in a saving's bank, so as to provide against an evil day, and also the formation of an association to promote the general advancement and improvement of the working classes, and to collect information on all matters affecting their interests, and to prevent the expatriation of Canadians. This is an interesting and useful address, but Mr. Parent introduces extraneous matter, in a way to weary the reader.

Discours consists of two lectures: the first is on "Intellect and its relations to society," and the second, "An elaboration of a project of law, alluded to in the first." Mr. Parent begins by protesting against the separation of religion from political society; he believes there should be union. Although he does not advocate the amalgamation of church and state, each should work in unison, within its own circle to the same end—the moral, intellectual and material advancement of mankind. God teaches us in historical facts, " that the hand which bears the censor, should not wield the sceptre." To the church belong counsel and warning; to the state legislation and the direct governing of society; to the church to point out the way; and to the state, to tread therein; and finally, to the people to follow. Mr. Parent asserts that man should be governed by the higher intellects of society. The sovereignty of the masses he characterizes as the sovereignty of blind instinct; good and generous at times, but ever unreasonable, and which must result in "anarchy and confusion." The masses are incapable of forming just or enlightened opinions on political science, and they are sure to be made the tools of the designing. As to hereditary government, it is incompetent to maintain intellect at the head of society; to insure it, intellect should also be hereditary, which, as all know, is far from being the case. Representative government is but a step in the right direction. The law of subordination of the inferior to the superior being is that of the whole of creation. All revolutions, he contends, originate with men of great intellectual attainments, who, being dissatisfied with society, and balked of their ambition, seek to rise through the prejudices of the masses. As a remedy to this evil, he suggests, to open up new fields of venture and horizons to this class to remove the many obstacles, placed in their way by the *régime héréditaire*, and thus divert their abilities into channels which may be of benefit to themselves and to humanity. Until the political and social institutions recognize the sovereignty of intellect, directly and indirectly, the goal of a satisfactory form of government, shall not have been reached. He thinks the state should acknowledge its inability to cope with pauperism, and leave the poor to the care of religious bodies, who understand how to alleviate and prevent human miseries. Each citizen therefore, should be at the call of these bodies, and give all he can for that purpose ; those who can not be relieved, he would leave to the mercy of God "wh~se will it is that such should exist." (*ic*) The desire that there should be no suffering is very laudable ; but many, if they were sure of even a bare sustenance, would become idle and criminal. From such miseries we may derive a precious lesson—that there is good even in the trials sent us by Providence. Intellect is the only means of peacefully attaining the highest happiness permitted to man. He concludes by a project of a law, for the purpose of establishing an aristocracy of intellect, including a scheme of free primary education, and superior education for those, deemed worthy by their talents and good conduct ; also assistance to poor children, who, to follow the higher classes, have to be sent elsewhere.

Some of these schemes have long been carried out both here and abroad.

He also proposes money advances, reimbursable, with or without interest, to poor students of the superior grades, who, not receiving public appointments, desire to follow some profession, art or industry.

Even as it is, with strict examinations and heavy fees, the professions are overcrowded with young men, whose prospects might have been much brighter, had they been les. ambitious. With such premiums, we should have the country filled with briefless lawyers, patientless doctors, and deedless notaries.

Mr. Parent proposes an aristocracy of intellect, but the author thinks there would be difficulty in the practical working of his scheme, and in this I certainly agree with him, for his favored "Learned Society" would not long be tolerated in the practical age in which we live.

Supposing for a moment the possibility of the existence of a "Learned" class; the institution, being the creature of and supported by the government, it should, at least, have some control and the provision, that after a certain period, the central board should be appointed by itself, would work badly as in time it would find itself opposed to the government.

One of the rather questionable means of carrying out the objects of this fanciful scheme proposed is a fund to be made up of taxes on " heritages, legacies, gifts and donations *entre vifs*, which in cases of fraud shall be confiscated for its benefit."

It may be noticed that only the male sex is named for these advantages, but in case the author should be considered unjust, he says in regard to the fair sex, "before ornamenting a building, one must lay the foundations, complete the carpenter work and cover in the roof; that being done, it will be my first care to improve the condition of daughters of the people, which has not yet been done."

Doubtless, at the time the above schemes were proposed,

they were considered by many remarkable and sensible, but to-day they will be pronounced visionary and impracticable.

Mr. Parent's style is verbose and monotonous at times, suffering from the attempt to maintain a long and connected line of thought and work out a chain of reasoning to a correct conclusion. His addresses bear more the character of lectures of a college professor than of the discourses of a learned academician. Elegant diction appears with him a secondary consideration; some passages, however, are stamped with originality and force.

Voyages is the name of a small work by our national historian, F. X. Garneau, dedicated to the late Dr. Blanchet, a distinguished humanitarian and physician of this city. In the introduction, the author gives a rapid sketch of a trip he made, through Canada and the United States, when he visited the principal places of interest in both countries. He sails from Quebec, in 1831, and in due course of time arrives in London, after a pleasant voyage, during which he read Byron, Prior and Newton, in order to familiarize himself with the English language. When in the metropolis he visits Westminster Abbey and speaks of the great and honored dead lying buried there in an appropriate strain. In the House of Commons he hears O'Connell, Lord John Russell, Sir Robert Peel, Hume, Roebuck and a host of other celebrities, of whom he gives his impressions. He is much impressed by the oratory of O'Connell, and draws a comparison between the styles of English and French orators. The marked division of classes in society and its contrast with the equality in America give him much food for reflection. Stage coaching in England and *diligence* traveling in France are referred to, and read oddly in our days of steam and telegraph. Among the *literati* Mr. Garneau mentions having met the poet Campbell ; he also alludes to M. Paulin Guérin, the eminent painter, and M. Broussais, the celebrated theoretic physician. Since the days of the author's journey traveling has greatly altered; iron roads have shortened distances, and few would be tempted now to write such a book of travels. Mr. Garneau was at the time but twenty-two years of age, and was shortly afterwards appointed private secretary to M. D. B. Viger, the agent of Lower Canada in London. When in London the author had the pleasure of meeting several of his countrymen, eminent statesmen and writers. In feeling terms he alludes to the death of M. Bédard, after which the reader is treated to the home journey.

I am told by one who knows that Mr. Garneau was not by any means satisfied with this little volume, which first appeared in *Le Journal de Québec*. It is nevertheless a curious book to read, if only for the purpose of comparing the past with the present and to enable the reader to become acquainted with the varied emotions experienced by that young and brilliant mind. It is interesting to note his feelings as he witnesses the marvels of the old world and its civilization. Those desirous of forming an idea of Mr. Garneau's abilities his depth of knowledge and his wealth of illustration must read his *chef-d'œuvre*, *L'Histoire du Canada*.

Any notice of the works of *l'Abbé Ferland*, who enjoyed fame as a savant and a writer, would be incomplete which did not mention his master-piece, *Histoire du Canada*. Though his contributions to our literature on a variety of subjects, at different times, were works of no little merit, his history surpasses them all, whether the learning it displays, its author's industry, or the clearness and purity of style, be considered. It contains a vast amount of information respecting the earlier periods of our history; and historians have frequently consulted it for its valuable data and facts. The author's scholarly tastes, zeal for education and patriotic feeling were most conspicuously displayed during a long and honored career. All his works may be read with profit.

Louis-Olivier Gamache, by Mr. Ferland, is a short biography of a noted character. Formerly, those who were shipwrecked on the coast of Anticosti, even if they escaped with their lives, were doomed to death from hunger or cold. But new lighthouses have been the means of preventing many accidents and saving precious lives. The Abbé visits Gamache at his residence, on the bay bearing his name, where he receives a cordial welcome from his eccentric host, who was at that time sixty-eight years of age, but still hale, hearty and active. After a short conversation, the author's prejudices against him vanish and he finds him a rough but kind-hearted man. He amuses his host by detailing the general impressions concerning him; that he was looked upon as a pirate, a bandit, a wrecker and familiar with evil spirits. Gamache afterwards acknowledges that he purposely resorted to mystery and other means to create such beliefs for his own protection, as he was often exposed to attack from evil-disposed persons. The following details were supplied by Gamache to the author: At the early age of eleven he had served as a cabin-boy on board of an English frigate; when his time of service had expired he commenced his solitary life at Anticosti. He married, but so dreary and desolate an existence was unsuitable to the poor woman, who died within a year. He married a second time and had two children; but, on returning home one day, after an absence of two weeks, he found his helpmate dead, and clinging to her stiff and icy body were his two children, perishing from cold and hunger. He requests his guest to secure him another wife in Quebec, but this commission of "trust and honor" is respectfully declined by the Abbé. His house is strongly fortified, so as to stand a siege against any wandering, maliciously inclined characters, and firearms of every description are hung up in all the apartments. In 1854, Gamache was found dead in his house, as were his two wives before him. In his own words : " The devil is not always as black as he is painted," in which conclusion the author joins.

Fragment de l'Histoire du Canada—1759. This is a short sketch of the ravages by the British forces on the *Côte de Beaupré* at the time of Wolfe's siege of the city of Quebec. Mr. Ferland relates the reception at the village of Château Richer of the first news of the arrival of the hostile English fleet and the instructions of the Bishop of Quebec that they should take to the woods, which advice was acted upon immediately. When the English soldiers arrived they found but empty dwellings. These were burned, as also the churches, and everything of value which had been left behind was taken or consumed by fire. Thus were destroyed the villages of St. Joachim, Ste. Anne, Château Richer and L'Ange Gardien, by the men under command of captain Montgomery. Sixteen years afterwards, says the author, an English officer whilst examining the ruins of the monastery at the village of Château Richer, asked a bystander for information. He was Gravel and willingly related the story, when both were surprised that each had been an actor in the scene, for the English officer was in charge of the men who had attempted to take Gravel prisoner when reconnoitring. The former had arrived from England in the hope of meeting another old acquaintance, captain Montgomery, who was about besieging Quebec. This incident is charmingly related by the Abbé, but it is certain the Montgomery who is charged with cruelties on the *Côte de Beaupré* and general Montgomery of the American army who invested the ancient capital of Quebec, are not one and the same individual.

The next paper entitled *Labrador* is an account of a trip to that dreary coast, by the reverend author in July 1858, to visit the Catholics there resident. He reaches Berthier by steamer and there takes the schooner " Marie Louise " for the continuation of his voyage. They are but a few days out when in a storm they lose their mizenmast, which obliges them to put into Mingan, a trading post of the Hudson Bay Company, with a large and safe harbor, one hundred and thirty leagues below Quebec for repairs. The people of the lower St. Lawrence engage in seal-fishing in the early spring, which is followed by cod, herring and salmon fishing. The seals, he says, are killed by a heavy blow on the nose; they are found on fields of floating ice, in great numbers, and fishermen are careful to first despatch those ear the water's edge, for, were these to become alarmed and jump into the water the rest would follow and escape ; but, so long as these do not move, the others look on and are easily killed. The author also relates the history of Labrador: it was visited by Norwegians and Danes as early as the thirteenth century, and in 1497, by Jean and Sabastien Cabot. In 1500 Cortereal, a Portuguese, landed here, and from 1504 Basque fishermen from Normandy and Brittany fished in its waters. Up to 1800, no white woman had lived on the coast. At the time of Mr. Ferland's visit, women were few compared with the men, and married at a very early age, generally at fifteen. When a woman becomes ill, she must go to a neighbor's house, several miles away, to be attended by one of her sex there and her children accompany her. From Mingan to St. Augustin French is mostly spoken ; but from the latter place to Brador English is universal. There are few Indians or Esquimaux; but the people have adopted many of the habits of the latter, necessitated by the climate. At Natagamiou and Tête-à-la-Baleine, snow is found in the ravines and icebergs floating in the river in September. The hospitality of the people is most liberal ; strangers find open house everywhere. In the absence of the families dwellings are left open and supplied with provisions and occasionally money for accidental visitors. He gives full descriptions of the Esquimaux dogs, their habits and peculiarities and invaluableness in these regions. They, however, kill almost all other domestic animals; including cows, pigs and sheep. In summer, Esquimaux dogs are useless, but in winter, they are the sole means of communication, and haul immense loads—six or seven can draw three persons twenty to twenty-five leagues a day—and the storm-belated traveler may trust to the intelligence of these animals in the wildest hurricanes and blinding snow drifts to bring him safely to his house, or welcome shelter. The harpooning of whales and similar operations are described, as is also the herring fishery. At Grosse Isle are countless numbers of birds' nests filled with eggs, which are stolen and shipped to the United States and elsewhere and sold at great profit. Touching at Chickapoué, the author next lands at St. Augustin, where an extensive peltry trade is carried on; the most valuable furs being the silver and black fox skins. At Blanc Sablon there are extensive fishery establishments, and here the author notices the hitherto unexplained and extraordinary phenomenon of ice forming on the bed of the river, known as *glace du fond*, at a depth of fifty or sixty feet.

The style of the Abbé Ferland is clear, correct and lively; always pleasing, especially by its tone of good humor and French enthusiasm. There is nothing labored about his writings, which are sprightly and without effort. He does not make use of the artifice of antithesis, or of tinkling words, so much resorted to by the modern school in France; but his ideas spring from a pure source and flow sparklingly like a clear stream from a rock over a pebbly bed.

Discours prononcé 18 *Juillet*, 1855, *par L'Honorable P. J. O. Chauveau.* This oration was delivered on the occasion of the ceremony of laying the corner-stone of the monument erected to the memory of those who fell on the Plains of Abraham, 28th April, 1760. Mr. Chauveau declares that his words are but the feeble echoes of what must be the thoughts of all present, surrounded as they were by civil and military pomp, on ground saturated with the best blood of France and England. At the foot of this monument which was destined to proclaim to coming ages the glories of our ancestors, amid a scenery of the grandest, and the mind teeming with historical reminiscences, one could not help feeling a glow of patriotic pride. On the 28th April, six months after Wolfe and Montcalm had fallen, the one shrouded in the victorious flag of England, and the other in the banner bearing the immortal name of Carillon, another French army stood on the same battle field of the 13th September previous, an army whose ranks were filled with patriotic volunteers, some of whom had fought at Monongahela, Fort George, Oswego, and Carillon. It was grand on the part of the British army to defend their dearly won citadel; it was equally grand for the French troops, weakened by a long march, under tempestuous rain and thunder, but for the Canadian militia it was the final burial or the resurrection of all they had loved and venerated in their homes. For three hours the contest raged, and more than three thousand were left on the field of battle, their blood mingling with the snow and flooding the frozen ground. On this very spot, where once stood Dumont's mill, there was frightful mutual slaughter; the mill was three times taken. The Canadian militia furiously attacked the British centre, while the left wing was turned by the Canadians and Indians, throwing them back on the centre, and thus deciding the fate of the day. In presence, he said, of an English Governor and of British troops, before the Commandant of a French *Corvette*, in the midst of our fellow-citizens, English, Irish, Scotch, among the children of our old Huron allies, we, the descendants of the militiamen of 1760, deposit under the same monument, the bones of the Queen's Grenadiers, the Scotch Highlanders and other regiments, who fought on that memorable day, blessed by an archbishop, irrespective of the creed to which they belonged. Mr. Chauveau eloquently asks of posterity, what higher tribute could be paid to the heroism of ancient times, what more profound teaching offered than the erection of this monument, beneath which are the dead of two rival armies, in a common tomb, the wars and hatred of a past age being succeeded by the friendship and alliance of another? Finally he apostrophizes the dead warriors, beseeching them to rest quietly in their glory till they rise to a triumph not such as we feeble mortals can give, but a triumph without end and without bound, to commence by the grand review, which God will hold, when time shall be no more.

In this oration Mr. Chauveau revels in depicting the glories of the past, and chivalrously dwells upon the illustrious deeds of the heroic dead, according to all, regardless of race or creed, their just meed of praise. His purity of style is only equalled by the poetical color and elegant form of his thoughts.

LA LITTÉRATURE CANADIENNE
DE 1850 A 1860.

This second volume offers more variety than the previous, containg selections in verse as well as in prose, and will materially assist in spreading a knowledge of the literature of the country. It opens with several poems from the pen of the late Mr. Octave Crémazie. In national and war themes, the author is, *par excellence*, the poet of Canada, patriotism, ardent admiration of French glory and inspiring battle-cries characterizing his verse throughout. Of such are most of the pieces in this volume ; they are thoroughly heart-stirring, and to French-Canadians are suggestive of deeds of glory and chivalry. This martial spirit changes to a temper perfectly peaceful in "*Les Morts*" in which is expressed the happy calm of those lying beneath the sod, untroubled by the contentions of life and the raging of the storm above them. These departed spirits however reappear and lament the forgetfulness of the living:

> " Et l'oubli des vivants, pesant sur votre tombe,
> Sur vos os décharnés plus lourdement retombe
> Que le plomb du cercueil."

He apostrophizes these ghostly visitors in a few plaintive stanzas, commencing:

> "Tristes, pleurantes ombres,
> Qui dans les forêts sombres,
> Montrez vos blancs manteaux
> Et jetez cette plainte
> Qu'on écoute avec crainte
> Gémir dans les roseaux."

Le Drapeau de Carillon gives a national retrospect of the martial glories of Canada and especially of the famous victory of Carillon and the following appeal is made:

> " Ah, bientôt puissions nous, ô drapeau de nos pères !
> Voir tous les Canadiens unis, comme des frères,
> Comme au jour du combat se serrer près de toi !
> Puisse des souvenirs la tradition sainte
> En régnant dans leur cœur, garder de toute atteinte,
> Et leur langue et leur foi ! "

A pretty little ode is addressed to *L'Alouette*, and another to *Le Printemps*. Two poems to the memory of Monseigneur de Laval are deeply imbued with national and religious feeling. In *Les Mille Isles*, the poet first gives as a contrast a lively sketch of the old world attractions and beauties, but returns to Les Mille Isles as infinitely beyond any of its charms.

Among the other authors in this volume are MM. L. H. Fréchette and Pamphile LeMay, from each of whom a single selection is given. Of *Alleluia* by the former, I have already expressed my appreciation; and *Le Retour* by the latter is a charming poetical effusion. The three names of our national poets having thus accidentally come together, I am induced to draw a comparison between them as to their respective merits.

Of these lyric singers, the poetic element is strongest in Crémazie. If, however, his verse be not so perfect or elegant as that of Fréchette, who has all the delicacy of modern versification, Crémazie, on the other hand, exhibits grander ideas. When the author of *Le Drapeau de Carillon* takes his lute and evokes from it his first notes, the great ideal of country rises before him, and, trembling with inspiration, he chants in a triumphant voice the drama of Canadian heroes. His sonorous verse flows rhythmically from its source, and the images, which he creates, are natural and calm, seeming as proud in their niches and as free from affectation as ancient marbles. If Fréchette be less lyrical, he is a greater artist than Crémazie. His verse is occasionally as finished as that of Théophile Gauthier. But it may be this high finish, sometimes oppressive in form, which gives to the poet a portion of his strength. In his later compositions, his sonnets for instance, some of the stanzas are weak. Brilliant and sonorous words are wedded to frivolous ideas; like a necklace of pearls too heavy for the string which holds them and which may break at any moment. It must not be supposed, however, that Fréchette is wanting in imagination; in his two pieces on "Jolliet" and "Papineau," he rises to the highest flights to which the muse may soar.

LeMay sings of nature in a clear and tender voice, re-

ERRATUM.

The printers through error transposed from page 190, 21st line, after the words "Théophile Gauthier" to page 191, 7th line, the following sentence, "The *Emaux et Camées* have frequently been taken as his model."

loses a portion of its charm. His creations evince originality and beauty of form, but lack that modern finish and felicity of expression which often redeem mere commonplace conceptions. Thus, in brief, I have endeavored to give my appreciation of the styles of these three poets.

Le Chercheur de Trésors, by Philippe Aubert de Gaspé, *fils*, is the first prose selection in this work. Though without elaborate plot, this tale contains a few sketches and narratives of the supernatural that excite attention. At the opening, the author gives a description of an alchemist in search of the philosopher's stone, with the single selection is given. Of *Alleluia* by the former, I have already expressed my appreciation ; and *Le Retour* by the latter is a charming poetical effusion. The three names of our national poets having thus accidentally come together. I am induced to draw a comparison be-

drama of Canadian heroes. His sonorous verse flows rhythmically from its source, and the images, which he creates, are natural and calm, seeming as proud in their niches and as free from affectation as ancient marbles. If Fréchette be less lyrical, he is a greater artist than Crémazie. His verse is occasionally as finished as that of Théophile Gauthier. But it may be this high finish, sometimes oppressive in form, which gives to the poet a portion of his strength. In his later compositions, his sonnets for instance, some of the stanzas are weak. Brilliant and sonorous words are wedded to frivolous ideas; like a necklace of pearls too heavy for the string which holds them and which may break at any moment. It must not be supposed, however, that Fréchette is wanting in imagination; in his two pieces on "Jolliet" and "Papineau," he rises to the highest flights to which the muse may soar.

LeMay sings of nature in a clear and tender voice, reminding one of Alfred de Vigny, and approaching the elegance and polish of that poet. *The Émaux et Camées*, have frequently been taken as his model. In words of melody, he celebrates the beauties of rural life and scenery. He is touching, pleasing and sympathetic. He knows his subject well; he has seen it, he has felt it, he has loved it; indeed he yields too much to inspiration and does not sufficiently finish his verse, nor does he fully enough develop his idea, so as to reap all its wealth; his poetry thus loses a portion of its charm. His creations evince originality and beauty of form, but lack that modern finish and felicity of expression which often redeem mere commonplace conceptions. Thus, in brief, I have endeavored to give my appreciation of the styles of these three poets.

Le Chercheur de Trésors, by Philippe Aubert de Gaspé, *fils*, is the first prose selection in this work. Though without elaborate plot, this tale contains a few sketches and narratives of the supernatural that excite attention. At the opening, the author gives a description of an alchemist in search of the philosopher's stone, with the usual result of failure, without diminished hope. *Une main de gloire*, the dried arm of a man who has been hanged, is necessary. Fortunately for the alchemist, though not for the victim, a neighbor kills a colporteur, whose body is washed up by the waves of the St. Lawrence and identified by a brother colporteur, Saint-Céran. The murderer is hanged and his corpse given to the dissecting room. Amand, the alchemist, purloins the required arm, and with it sets out with a companion to seek his fortune. They land below Bay St. Paul and are overheard making their plans, by two medical students, who then perpetrate a practical joke by setting them to dig for a supposed hidden treasure. They are, later, overtaken in a storm, in which Amand loses his companion and himself is picked up at sea and subsequently landed on the Island of Anticosti, where he lives for some years. He has not, however, lost his *main de gloire* and one day finds a treasure, through, he supposes, its virtue. Ultimately, with the money found, he escapes from the island and from the tyrannies of a cruel task-master.

During the journey of Amand and his companion towards Bay St. Paul, is given the legend of *Rose Latulippe*: On the night of a party at her father's house, Rose was induced by a stranger to dance with him after midnight of a *Mardi-gras*, a sin according to the rules of the Roman Catholic Church, and to promise to be his partner all that evening. The *curé* opportunely arrives and saves her from the arms of the stranger, Lucifer, who departs in scorn and rage; the hoofs of his steed, while waiting at the door, having melted the snow to the very ground.

Another legend is *L'Homme de Labrador*, where again the evil one figures. A lawless scamp is left on the barren coast of Labrador by the crew of the vessel on board of which he was, who would not tolerate his presence any longer, there to be left to get along as best he might. On the first night of his stay, to his horror, he is visited by the devil, which the curious in *diablerie* will doubtless read with morbid gratification. The prodigal remembers enough of his early religious training to call on his Maker to chase away the wicked one, vowing to beg, penitentially from door to door for the rest of his life. He is rendered unconscious through the excitement caused by the vision, remaining thus long enough to compel the dog through hunger, to eat boots, and other such indigestible *pabulum*. The effect of all this was to reduce a man of great strength to childish weakness and mental imbecility, This forms a good temperance tract, " points a moral and adorns a tale."

The main story then continues: Saint-Céran having received his medical deploma, settles in Quebec, and devotes his time and skill to its citizens. He subsequently claims the hand of Amelia, the daughter of Amand, who opportunely arrives from Anticosti and graciously gives his consent, which he had previously witheld. And the marriage takes place under the happiest omens and with pleasantest results—the orthodox finale.

In the preface Mr. de Gaspé states that *Le Chercheur de Trésors*, is the first novel treating of Canadian habits and customs, but I should hardly call it that, as it consists mainly of a string of anecdotes, not well connected either in circumstance or plot. His father, who afterwards published his well-known and fascinating works, deals with similar subjects with greater skill and attractiveness, and gives more animating representations of the life and features of the last century. The only chapter in this work which emits the true ring of his father's metal is *L'Homme de Labrador*, which, to a certain extent, impresses one, wit' out, however, liveliness or humor to relieve its darker side. The style is defective, but the work deserves perusal for its legendary stores.

There are two delightful little *pièces de vers*, by Felix G. Marchand, late minister of Crown Lands in Hon. Mr. Joly's government, *La Jeune Mère au chevet de son Fils*, and *Le Printemps*. It is unfortunate that political life should have deprived literature of further graceful compositions from this gentleman. He has written a comedy, *L'Erreur n'est pas Com.'e*, replete with good hits and *bons mots*, displaying versatility of talent and imagination. I hope Mr. Marchand will again adorn literature with his writings. In the *Histoire de la Littérature Cana-*

dienne, by Edmond Lareau, a work of varied merits, the author thus expresses himself in reference to Mr. Marchand : " *C'est un véritable littérateur, le type du journaliste gentilhomme.*"

Importance des Études Religieuses. This is the title of two lectures delivered at St. Hyacinthe by M. l'Abbé J. S. Raymond, Vicar-General, in which the above subject is discussed. The author insists that religious instruction is essential, and that if it were abandoned, morality, from which alone it springs, must also be doomed. He combats the pretentions of the socialists and communists and impugns the truth of their tenets, and states that, whenever such views take possession of the mind, there is sure to follow moral bankruptcy. He argues that if religious truth is the living principle of the well-being of society, this truth, as it is, should be recognized as its precepts. Religion should not be considered as a subject apart, in that it has but the firmer dominion over the intelligence of the world ; and he continues, that there is in the separation of religion, from other objects of human knowledge an "inconceivable error," an essential fault in logic, a total failure of thought on the destiny of the intellectual faculties. All wars, dissensions, discussions and conflicts were the result in a society without unity of the principles of true order. If the existence of society is divinely established, no political, nor civil institution should be permitted to oppose it. The study of religion should, therefore, furnish the solution of many of the great problems of social and political economy. Religion says that the will emanates from God, and if society have a right to transmit or curtail its liberty, its interests demand the respect and preservation of the constituted authorities. The author, from these broad questions, then investigates those affecting communities, private parties and family relations. He concludes by inciting the religious souvenirs, which attach to one's native country.

These are clever treatises on the subject of social morality and its political relations, and few could be more competent to dilate thereon than l'Abbé Raymond. His thoughts bear the impress of careful reflection and are clearly and succinctly laid before the reader. He is an eminent educationalist who has rendered great services to his district.

Those who have read the choice poetry of Mr. L. J. C. Fiset will be pleased to meet in this book a few of the more especial favorites. *Les Voix du Passé, Méditations, Le Poète à la Muse,* and *Le Vœu de Mariette* are to be found here. This poet's verse is generally pleasing, free and unaffected, his themes being graceful. He was wrong in deserting the muse so early; in continuing to court her, he might have acquired greater strength, more amplitude and color.

The next piece of prose is an interesting description of Naples and its environs, by N. Bourassa, in which, of course, are given the ascent to Mount Vesuvius and a visit to the ever attractive subterranean cities of Pompeii and Herculaneum. But I can not attempt to mention the different places of historic fame, visited by the author. There are many artistic details concerning objects of art that will charm many a reader. They are evidently written by a *connaisseur.*

There are published here *Misère, La Fenêtre Ouverte, Le Roi des Aulnes*, by J. Lenoir. This gentleman's early death was a great loss to our literature. There is a softness and tenderness in the verse of this poet, which render his effusions particularly charming to certain natures. His flights are never bold, but he agreeably describes scenery, the beautiful azure and the harmonious notes of nature. He was a modest reflex of the school of 1830, which bequeathed to France, so many delightful literary souvenirs. Several passages are in imitation of Lamartine.

Premières Pages de la Vie, by Alfred Garneau, is a friendly missive in verse, in reply to a letter received from a friend. There is a perfume, a bouquet of heart qualities, such as is refreshing to read in our unsentimental, practical age. The emotions of his early years are revived, recalling similar experiences in the minds of his readers and making them long for their repetition. The few pieces of his poetry which I have seen are of a nature to cause regret that he has written so little. His verse has a warmth his images a reality a piquant originality, while his language is of the purest and most correct kind. His stanzas are highly polished and are fine stones in a setting of pure gold—charming little gems. This gentleman is presently engaged in re-editing the *Histoire du Canada* of his father's, with copious notes and additions.

Mr. Adelard Bouchard, in a few well written pages, *Une Page de notre Histoire*, gives an account of the troubles of 1812, when French-Canadians covered themselves with glory in vanquishing the foes of England. At that time, the Roman Catholic Church authorities, at Montreal, issued a circular, in which their flock were exhorted to patriotism towards England, to support British power and battle the enemy, and were addressed in the following terms: " Great Britain alone, glorying in a thousand rays, stood amidst overturned thrones; a power which never engaged in battle but for victory, which never attacked a fortress but to gain it, which never undertook the defence of a weak country but to render it invincible." In this way the martial ardor of the people was aroused, and their valor on the field testified to their bravery, faith and homage.

A la Gloire de Pie IX by Zéphyrin Mayrand closes this interesting and well selected collection of Canadian literature.

I would fain review the few remaining works of the department, but I have reached my prescribed limit. Should the " Literary Sheaves " meet with anything like liberal encouragement, I shall in a subsequent edition include them and others that may be published in the meantime.

THE MARQUIS OF LORNE'S ACADEMY PROJECT.

Decori decus addit avito.

At a period when the original design of this work had been fully accomplished and the author's task in connection with it almost concluded, I read with pleasure an able article in the "Quebec Morning Chronicle" from the pen of its editor, Mr. George Stewart, Jr., so well and favorably known both in the Dominion and the United States, in which was mentioned the desire of His Excellency the Governor General the Marquis of Lorne, to establish a Canadian Academy, after the model of *L'Académie Française*, which has rendered such valuable services to the literature, arts and sciences of that country. I am happy of the present opportunity of expressing my gratification at the well-timed interest in Canadian literature, which the representative of Her Majesty has manifested. Such an idea is worthy of its exalted source and encouragingly advances the purpose of my reviews, namely: the revealing to the English speaking public the treasures and resources of French-Canadian literature. I have long regarded it as unfortunate that the former should know so little of the varied and *spirituel* writings of the latter, and that these on their part should also exhibit apathy to our fast-growing and promising English literature.

For this indifference and denial of merited encouragement to our authors there is no excuse, when so many foreign productions, inferior to Canadian works, receive liberal patronage. An Academy or Association, based upon broad and liberal principles, and animated by a fraternal and patriotic spirit, could not fail of accomplishing much needed and highly beneficial work, creditable to our national feelings and tastes, and fraught with the brightest promise to our literature. To the consummation of this end petty professional jealousies and unworthy prejudices should be discouraged, in favor of a spirit of mutual appreciation and sympathy among our writers, who need all the usual and material support obtainable in a country of the scant population and limited resources of the Dominion. Everything to improve the circumstances and cheer the labors of our literary classes should be heartily undertaken, not only on sentimental and artistic, but on progressive grounds, as a flourishing literature cannot fail of increasing the laudable pride of Canadians in their country, enhancing its reputation abroad and making known in the most effective manner its valuable stores.

This *entente cordiale* once established, the founding of a Canadian nation, with the disappearance of all sectional feelings, would naturally follow. As early as 1832, a

French-Canadian philanthropist and patriot, Joseph François Perrault, in a pamphlet entitled *Moyens de conserver Nos Institutions, Notre Langue et Nos Lois*, entreated all parties " to unite and form one single nation, having the same institutions, obeying the same laws and striving to uphold the glory of the British Empire and the prosperity of the colony." To attain such a result should be the aim of all true patriots, and indirectly the formation of the proposed association would tend to that end. Among other advantages, which might be enumerated, would be the facility with which we could unite with similar societies in the United States and other countries, to secure an international copyright, a subject of deep importance to all authors.

In this country, as in most colonies, literature is not followed as a profession, but rather as a diversion, except by the fourth estate; the daily wants of life compelling those of such tastes to consider the *res angusta domi*. Both races look to their respective mother-countries for mental inspiration and sustenance; their thoughts and styles being influenced and guided by works from the other side of the Atlantic. We lack not talent, but we are deficient in boldness and originality; and the stimulating and emulating influences of such a society will enable us in the course of a short time to found a characteristic, national and independent literature.

It is not surprising to those who know His Excellency's

high endowments and accomplishments, that so enlightened a project should have emanated from him, even amid the important and absorbing duties and cares of state. Should the success which I anticipate ensue from it, it must cast a halo of literary renown on his administration. In the Marquis' wish to establish a nucleus of Canadian literature, we have the assurance of not merely a temporary interest, to end with his term of office, but a permanent one bound up with the friendliest of intentions towards Canada. A disposition of this kind, on the part of one surrounded by social distractions, proves him worthy of his origin, as well as the very important position he occupies. From no higher source could proceed a more encouraging project to Canadian *belles-lettres* than from a member of the house of Argyle, which enjoys a patent of nobility, not only of birth, but of intellect and statesmanship greater even than that political distinction, which it has so long worthily maintained. His Excellency in this undertaking gives evidence of tastes similar to those of his noble father, whose fame as a scholar and statesman is of the highest rank. A writer himself, he evinces a fraternal feeling towards the literary craft, as well as a desire of doing what may lie in his power to promote the intellectual and general interest of the country. In response to such a promising suggestion, and in the hope of realizing to the fullest extent its author's praiseworthy objects, the people of Canada should promptly extend to the Marquis their heartiest co-operation.

With regard to the success of this scheme, much will depend upon the character of the organization proposed, but more upon the spirit of its members. Should it manifest candor, liberality and mutual respect, he would be bold indeed who would attempt to limit its sphere of usefulness. M. Paul de Cazes, in a clever and practical article on this subject to *L'Èvénement*, proposes to adopt a constitution similar to that of the Council of Public Instruction of this province, and form two separate boards, one of each nationality, to regulate ordinary questions of internal economy, and which would act conjointly when subjects of general interest would be under discussion. This system would prevent the possibilitity of any feeling of discontent, which might arise from partiality in the distribution of prizes, when the competency of one was disputed by the other in their judgment of literary works. In a community like ours, where there are different creeds and nationalities, some rule should be adopted, which, while preserving intact the rights of each class, would avoid offending the susceptibilities of all.

I would propose that the membership should have a proportion according to population in reference to nationality, and selected from among the most eminent of our *littérateurs* and scientists. Also that in the prizes to be awarded there should be certain sums placed at the disposal of the two boards, and in proportion, and to be granted by them to their different nationalities ; and further, there should be a fund under the control of the united board, to be distributed as prizes to contestants on subjects open to all. In reference to the name this society should bear, and which has given rise to much correspondence, I would say that this and other details can be hereafter settled. At any rate the interests of the minority, the French-Canadians, might safely be entrusted to the Marquis, whose sympathy towards them has been so often manifested.

The association would come into life under the happiest auspices, every youth feeling especially bound to set before his mind a high ideal in connection with its objects and efforts, and acknowledgment of the enlightenment, patriotism and high aims of its distinguished founder, who deserves the classic compliment, *nihil quod tetigit non ornavit*, which, I hope, may ere long become a well-merited tribute of the new organization itself.

> "Their cause I plead,—plead it in heart and mind;
> A fellow-feeling makes one wondrous kind."
> —DAVID GARRICK.

I sincerely hope that the publication of the preceding literary notices and reviews, brief and imperfect though they be, will in some measure increase the knowledge of the public, particularly the nationalities in the Dominion, unacquainted with the French language, who will thus be taught to think more highly of their fellow-subjects, using that medium of thought and expression, and experience a spirit of generous emulation, which may cause them to contribute more liberally to the mental treasures of the nation. Anything promotive of popular education, anything stimulative of thought, fancy and literary ambition, must be productive of good, in those higher regions upon which intellectual advancement and true civilization mainly depend. Mental pleasures and progress have ever been deemed objects of the utmost value and advantage—desirable in themselves, as well as for their fruits, by the leaders of mankind and the patriots of every clime and age. I am encouraged by the reflection, that such efforts are being appreciated by a section of our French speaking fellow-citizens, who, while recognizing the claims of English literature and the duties of their position as fellow-workers with the British, in the creation of a great

Canadian nation, have shown a marked interest in the development of a pure, healthy and animating French literature. Already its achievements merit our highest commendation. It has created a world of romance and chivalry, strewn its fields with the brightest and most fragrant flowers of fancy, and peopled its hills and dales with heroes beyond the power of time to destroy. By the magic wand of the poet, of the novelist, of the historian, the long, dead, forgotten past revives in all its impressive reality, with all its bewildering charms; its *bizarre* colors, its weird features, its strange, mysterious habits and customs; its striking characters reappear in their interesting or startling parts; its heroes, sinners and martyrs once more present their familiar faces, venerable with age, on this antique stage, to reproduce the old effects and to re-enact their ancient *rôles*. The past is thus made the back-ground of the present, its contrast and its inspiration. Noble lives are again made to impress their eloquent lessons, base natures again to ring their doleful warnings. Art, too, has its worthy mission in these intellectual achievements; its rules must guide the writer, who would win success. The heroes of the imagination must appear in life-like colors and proportions; reason must guide their speech and actions; while the poet weaves his fancies and builds his airy castles by rules older than the pyramids. Thus are the faculties of mankind developed, instructed and strengthened; thus art advances, and civilization extends her healing, refining influences. Much as has already been done by the present generation of Canadian writers to build up a national literature, it is to be hoped that the next, profiting by the example and achievements of the present, will make vast additions to the noble edifice, till by the purity of its style, the strength of its material and the grandeur of its proportions, it may symbolize the great Canadian nation to be and command the homage of the intellectual world.

FINIS.

INDEX

A

Agriculture L', dans la Province de Québec, - - - - 57
Association L', de Médecine Canadienne, - - - - 58
Anciens Les, Canadiens, - - - - - - - 63
A la Veillée, Contes et Récits, - - - - - - 72
Amiral L', du Brouillard, - - - - - - 75
Amérique L', avant Christophe Colombe, - - - - 110
Affaire L', Guibord, - - - - - - - - 112
Après le Combat, - - - - - - - - 116
A travers la Vie, - - - - - - - - 145
A mes Enfants, - - - - - - - 147
Au Coin du Feu, - - - - - - - - 149

B

Bois, Abbé E. D., - - - - - - - 69
Buies, Arthur, - - - - - - - - 129
Bienville, François de, - - - - - - - 142
Bouchard, Adélard, - - - - - - - - 198

C

Chauveau, Hon P. J. O., - - - - - - 9
Casgrain, Abbé, L', - - - - - - - - 39
Coup d'Œil sur l'Etat Actuel de la Médecine, - - - 60

Chansons d'Enfants, - - - - - - - 61
Crucifix Le, Outragé, - - - - - - 75
Crémazie, Octave, - - - - - - 105–188
Chroniques, - - - - - - - - 133
Chevalier Le, de Mornac, - - - - - - 139
Collier Le, Bleu de Mariette, - - - - - 147
Chasse Une, à l'Ours, - - - - - - 149
Canada Le, en Europe, - - - - - - 150
Canada Le, Sous l'Union, - - - - - - 153
Canadiens Les, de l'Ouest, - - - - - 167
Considérations sur les Classes Ouvrières, - - - - 172
Chercheur Le, de Trésors, - - - - - 191
Canadian The, Academy, - - - - - - 200

D

Défricheur Le, de Langue, tragédie-bouffe, - - - 53
Discours de Fin d'Année, - - - - - - 154
Danses Rondes, - - - - - - - 60
De Gaspé, Philippe Aubert, - - - - - 63
Dambourgès, Colonel, - - - - - - - 60
Dodo l'Enfant, - - - - - - - 74
Deux Ans au Mexique, - - - - - - 78
Dunn, Oscar, - - - - - - - 106
Dix Ans de Journalisme, - - - - - - 112
Dorion, Hon. A. A., - - - - - - 123
De Cazes, Paul, . - - - - - - 160
Discours, - - - - - - - - 173
Discours par l'honorable P. J. O. Chauveau, - - 185
De Gaspé, Philippe Aubert, *fils,* - - - - 191

E

Education,	2
Education in Ontario,	12
Education in Quebec,	12
Educational Institutions,	15
Evangile L', Prêchée,	22
Eloge Funèbre de l'Abbé Louis-Jacques Casault,	54
Encan, L',	147

F

Fêtes Patronales des Canadiens-Français,	56
Faucher de Saint-Maurice,	72
Feu des Roussi, Le,	73
Fantôme de la Roche, Le,	74
Fréchette, L. H.,	102–189
Ferland, Abbé, L',	179
Fragment de l'Histoire du Canada,	181
Fiset, L. J. C.,	196

G

Gaspésie,	98
Glossaire Franco-Canadien,	127
Garneau, F. X.,	177
Gamache, Louis-Olivier,	180
Garneau, Alfred,	197

H

Héroïsme et Trahison,	135
Homme D', de Labrador,	193

I

Instruction L', publique au Canada, - - - 11-109-118
Ilet L', au Massacre, ou l'Evangile ignorée, - - - - 19
Iliade L', et la Médecine, - - - - - - 60
Ile d'Orléans, - - - - - - - - - 61
Il ne faut désespérer de rien, - - - - - - 145
Iroquois et Algonquins, - - - - - - - 150
Importance des Etudes Religieuses, - - - - - 195

J

Jongleuse La, - - - - - - - - - 46
Jean Nicolet, - - - - - - - - 150

L

Légendes Les, Canadiennes, - - - - - - 44
Larue, Professor Hubert, - - - - - - 51
Langue Française au Canada, - - - - - - 51
Luxe et Vanité - - - - - - - - 52
Le Moine, J. M., - - - - - - - - 23
Lectures pour tous, - - - - - - - 107
Loi Electorale La, - - - - - - - - 120
Laberge, Charles, - - - - - - - - 122
Le Moyne, famille, - - - - - - - - 144
La Nouvelle-France, - - - - - - - 145
Legendre, Napoléon, - - - - - - - 147
Le Loup-Garou, - - - - - - - - 149
La Littérature Canadienne, - - - - - 169-188
L'Importance et les Devoirs du Commerce, - - - 170

Labrador, - - - - - - - - - 182
LeMay, Pamphile, - - - - - - - - 189

M

Mouvement Littéraire et Intellectuel, - - - - 15
Mélanges d'Histoire, de Littérature et d'Economie Politique, - 51
Mémoires de M. de Gaspé, - - - - - - 55
Mon Ami Jean, - - - - - - - - - 74
Mexico, - - - - - - - - - - 76
Manuel de Dessin Industriel, - - - - - - 127
Marmette, Joseph, - - - - - - - 135
Mlle de Verchères, - - - - - - - - 135
Mort La, d'un Brave, - - - - - - - 143
Macchabées Les, de la Nouvelle-France, - - - - 143
Marchand, F. G., - - - - - - - - 194
Mayrand, Zéphyrin, - - - - - - - - 199

N

Notaires, Avocats et Médecins, - - - - - 53
Naufrage dans le Golfe St. Laurent, - - - - 55
Nos Gloires Nationales, - - - - - - 108
Notes sur le Canada, - - - - - - - 161

O

Ouïmet, Hon. Gédéon, - - - - - - - 4–163
Opuscules, - - - - - - - - - 40

P

Perrault, Joseph-François, - - - - - - 13–200
Pionniers Les, Canadiens, - - - - - - 40

Pélérinage à l'Ile aux Coudres, - - - - - 41
Paresse et Travail, - - - - - - - 52
Promenades dans le Golfe Saint-Laurent, - - - - 85
Provinces Maritimes, - - - - - - - 94
Pourquoi nous sommes Français, - - - - - 107
Pouvoir Temporel, - - - - - - - 108
Pétition au Ministre de l'Instruction Publique, - - - 118
Patois Canadien, - - - - - - - 125
Parent Etienne, - - - - - - - 169

Q

Quebec Past and Present, - - - - - - 24
Question Agricole, - - - - - - 119

R

Richesses Naturelles du Canada, - - - - - 56
Rose Latulippe, - - - - - - - 192
Raymond, Abbé L', J. S., - - - - - - 195

S

Ste. Foye, Monument des Braves, - - - - - 16
Sagamo du Kapskouk, - - - - - - 20
Scènes de Mœurs Canadiennes, - - - - - 60
Saguenay Le, et la Vallée du Lac St. Jean, - - 129
Sulte, Benjamin, - - - - - - - 149
Scholastic Institutions, - - - - - - 165

T

Taché, J. C., - - - - - - - 18
Trois Légendes de mon Pays, - - - - - 18

Tableau de la Rivière Ouelle, - - - - - - 45
Turcotte, Lucien, - - - - - - - - 124
Traitres et Braves, - - - - - - - 126
Tomahawk Le, et L'Epée, - - - - - - - 138
Turcotte, Louis P., - - - - - - - 153
Tassé, Joseph, - - - - - - - - - 167

U

Union L', des Catholiques, - - - - - - 113

V

Voyages, - - - - - - - - - - 177

www.ingramcontent.com/pod-product-compliance
Lightning Source LLC
Chambersburg PA
CBHW031814230426
43669CB00009B/1142